Marcus Dods

The Parables of Our Lord

Marcus Dods

The Parables of Our Lord

ISBN/EAN: 9783744761000

Printed in Europe, USA, Canada, Australia, Japan

Cover: Foto ©Lupo / pixelio.de

More available books at **www.hansebooks.com**

THE PARABLES OF OUR LORD

MARCUS DODS, D.D.

[*THE PARABLES RECORDED BY ST MATTHEW*]

NEW YORK: MACMILLAN & CO.

1883

CONTENTS.

CHAP.		PAGE
I.	THE SOWER	1
	Matt. xiii. 1-9, 18-23; Luke vii 4-15.	
II.	THE TARES	25
	Matt. xiii. 24-30, 36-43.	
III.	THE MUSTARD SEED	45
	Matt. xiii. 31, 32.	
IV.	THE LEAVEN	67
	Matt. xiii. 33.	
V.	THE HID TREASURE AND THE PEARL OF PRICE	89
	Matt. xiii. 44-46.	
VI.	THE NET	109
	Matt. xiii. 47-50.	
VII.	THE UNMERCIFUL SERVANT OR THE UNFORGIVING DEBTOR	129
	Matt. xviii. 23-35.	

CHAP.		PAGE
VIII.	LABOURERS IN THE VINEYARD. FIRST LAST AND LAST FIRST	151
	Matt. xx. 1-16.	
IX.	THE TWO SONS	171
	Matt. xxi. 28-32.	
X.	THE WICKED HUSBANDMEN	193
	Matt. xxi. 33-45.	
XI.	THE MARRIAGE OF THE KING'S SON	213
	Matt. xxi. 45—xxii. 14.	
XII.	THE TEN VIRGINS	233
	Matt. xxv. 1-13.	
XIII.	THE TALENTS	255
	Matt. xxv. 14-30.	

I.

THE SOWER.

"*The same day went Jesus out of the house, and sat by the s[ea] side. And great multitudes were gathered together unto him, [so] that he went into a ship, and sat; and the whole multitu[de] stood on the shore. And he spake many things unto them i[n] parables, saying, Behold, a sower went forth to sow; And wh[en] he sowed, some seeds fell by the way side, and the fowls came an[d] devoured them up: some fell upon stony places, where they ha[d] not much earth: and forthwith they sprung up, because they ha[d] no deepness of earth: and when the sun was up, they we[re] scorched; and because they had no root, they withered awa[y.] And some fell among thorns; and the thorns sprung up, an[d] choked them: but other fell into good ground, and brought fort[h] fruit, some an hundredfold, some sixtyfold, some thirtyfold. Wh[o] hath ears to hear, let him hear."* . . . *"Hear ye therefore th[e] parable of the sower. When any one heareth the word of th[e] kingdom, and understandeth it not, then cometh the wicked one, and catcheth away that which was sown in his heart. This i[s] he which received seed by the way side. But he that received th[e] seed into stony places, the same is he that heareth the word, an[d] anon with joy receiveth it; yet hath he not root in himself, bu[t] dureth for a while: for when tribulation or persecution ariseth because of the word, by and by he is offended. He also tha[t] received seed among the thorns is he that heareth the word; an[d] the care of this world, and the deceitfulness of riches, choke th[e] word, and he becometh unfruitful. But he that received seed int[o] the good ground is he that heareth the word, and understandeth it; which also beareth fruit, and bringeth forth, some an hundredfold, some sixty, some thirty."*--MATT. xiii. 1-9, 18-23.

THE SOWER.

MATT. xiii. 1-9, 18-23; LUKE vii. 4-15.

THIS parable had to be spoken. It gave expression to thoughts which burdened the mind of Jesus throughout His ministry. On the day He uttered it, He had left the house and was sitting by the sea-side, "and there were gathered unto Him great multitudes." He had no difficulty in finding an audience. It is one of the greatest pleasures to listen to a good speaker. It is a pleasure which attracts young and old, rich and poor, educated and uneducated. A good speaker is always sure of an audience, and especially where he has not to encounter the rivalry of books. But as Jesus watched the crowd assembling, and perceived the various dispositions with which the people came, He could not but reflect how much of what He had to say must certainly be lost on many. He knew He had that to tell men which, if received, would change the face of society, and turn the wilderness into a garden. He was conscious of that in His own mind which, could it only be conveyed into the minds of those pressing around Him, would cause their lives to flourish with righteousness, beauty, love, usefulness, and joy. He had "many things to say" to them, things that never yet had fallen and never again could fall from human lips; and yet who, of the thousands that listened, would believe? They came, some out of curiosity, some saying within themselves, "What will this sower of words say?" some out of hatred, seeking occasion against Him; but all thinking themselves entitled to hold and express an opinion regarding the importance or worthlessness of what He said. They needed to have their critical faculty exercised upon themselves, and to be reminded that in order to benefit by what He had to say, they must bring certain capacities.

The parabolic form of teaching is pleasant to listen to; it is easily retained in the memory; it stimulates thought, each man being left to find an interpretation for himself; and it avoids the offensiveness of direct rebuke. To the crowd Jesus speaks only of the sower in the fields, and makes no explicit reference to Himself or to them.

The object of this parable, then, is to explain the causes of the failure and success of the gospel. Apart from experience, it might have been supposed that our Lord had only to proclaim His kingdom in order to gather all men to His

ndard. If it were so that God desired all
[me]n to enter into everlasting joy, did not this
[rem]ove every difficulty, and secure the happi-
[nes]s of all? Could such a messenger and such
[a]message fail to move every one who came in
[con]tact with them? Alas! even after so many
[cen]turies Christianity is not the one only
[rel]igion men believe in; and even where it is
[pro]fessed, it is most inadequately under-
[sto]od and received. Why, then, is it so?
[Wh]y, to so lamentable an extent does every
[age]ncy for the extension of Christ's kingdom
[fail]? It fails, says our Lord, not because the
[cla]ims of the kingdom are doubtful, not because
[the]y are inappropriately urged—these causes
[ma]y no doubt sometimes operate — but the
[kin]gdom fails to extend because the fructifica-
[tio]n of the seed of the word depends upon the
[nat]ure of the soil it falls upon, and because that
[soi]l is often impervious, often shallow, often
[emp]ty. The seed is not in fault, the sowing is
[no]t in fault, but the soil is faulty—a statement
[of] the case as little accepted by those in our
[ow]n day who discuss Christ's claims, as it was
[by] our Lord's contemporaries.

1. The first faultiness of soil our Lord speci-
[fies] in the words, "Some seeds fell by the
[wa]yside, and the fowls came and devoured
[the]m up;" and the interpretation or spiritual
[an]alogue He gives in the words, "When any

one heareth the word of the kingdom and *understandeth it not*, then cometh the wicked one and catcheth away that which was sown in his heart." The beaten footpath that crosses the corn field, and that is maintained year after year, or the cart-track along the side of the field, may serve a very useful purpose, but certainly it will grow no corn. The hard surface does not admit the seed: you might as well scatter seed on a wooden table, or a pavement, or a mirror. The seed may be of the finest quality, but for all the purposes of sowing you might as well sprinkle pebbles or shot. It lies on the surface. This state of matters then represents that hearing of the word which manages to keep the word entirely outside. The word has been heard, but that is all. It has not even entered the understanding. It has been heard as men listen to what is said in a foreign language. The mind is not interested; it is roused to no enquiry, provoked to no contradiction. You have sometimes occasion to suggest a different course of action to a friend; and, in order to do so, you mention a fact which should be sufficient to alter his purpose, but you find he has not apprehended its significance, has not seen its bearing—it has not fructified in his mind as you expected, and you say to yourself, "He does not take it in." So says our Lord; there are hearers who do

THE SOWER. 7

…t take in what is said; they do not see the …arings of the word they hear; their understanding is impervious, impenetrable.

Are there such hearers? Surely there are. …here are persons on whom the seed of the …ord falls as by accident, and who have neither …repared themselves to hear it, nor make any …fort to retain it. They are members of a …urch-going family, or they have formed a …urch-going habit of their own; they have …erhaps their reason for being found side by …de with those who hear with profit, but they …o not come for the sake of hearing; they are …ot anxious to hear, thoughtful about what they …ear, careful to retain it. There are careless …ersons who hear the word not as the result of … decision that it *is* to be heard; not as they …ould, on beginning the study of chemistry or …f philosophy, seek out certain teachers and …ertain books; but as the hearing of the word …appens to be the employment of the hour, …hey submit to this social convention, and they …llow the seed of the kingdom to fall upon them …ith no more expectation than that with which …hey hear the passing salutation of a friend …n the street, knowing that whether he says it …s a fine day or not, it is equally without significance. This hearing of the word has come to …e one of the many employments with which …en fill up their time, and this hearer has never thought why, nor whether it does him any good or no. He has never considered why he personally should listen to this special kind of word, nor what he personally may expect as the result of it.

There are, in short, persons who, either from preoccupation with other thoughts and hopes, have their minds beaten hard and rendered quite impervious to thoughts of Christ's kingdom, or from a natural slowness and hard frostiness of nature, hear the word without admitting it even to work in their understanding. They do not ponder what is heard, they do not check the statements they hear by their own thought; they do not consider the bearings of the gospel on themselves. When you propose to a farmer who is paying too high a rent to go to some part of the country where rents are lower, the idea will probably find entrance into his understanding. He may not ultimately adopt it, but it will stir a great many hopes and thoughts of various kinds in him, and he will find his mind dwelling on it day after day, and hour by hour, so that he can speak of little else. But the proposals made to the wayside hearer suggest nothing at all to him. His mind throws off Christ's offers as a slated roof throws off hail. You might as well expect seed to grow on a tightly-braced drum-head as the word to profit such a hearer; it dances on the hard surface, and the slightest motion shakes it off.

The consequence is, it is forgotten. When seed is scattered on a hard surface it is not allowed to lie long. The birds devour it up. Every hedge, every tree, every roof contributes its eager few, and shortly not a corn remains. So when not even the mind has been interested in Christ's word, that word is quickly forgotten; the conversation on the way home from church, the thought of to-morrow's occupations, the sight of some one on the street—anything, is enough to take it clean away. In some persons the word is admitted though it does not at once bring forth fruit. As in the old fable the words spoken unheard in the Arctic circle were thawed into sound and became audible in warmer latitudes; so when a man passes into new circumstances and a state of life more congenial to the development of Christian discipleship, the word which has apparently been lost for years begins to stir and make itself heard in his soul. But it cannot be so with the wayside hearer, for in him the word has never found any manner of lodgment.

2. The second faultiness of soil our Lord enumerates is *shallowness*. What we commonly understand by "stony ground" is a field thickly strewn with small stones; not the best

kind of soil, but quite available for growing corn. This is not the soil meant here. Our Lord speaks rather of rocky ground, where a thin surface of mould overlies an impenetrable rock. There is a mere dusting of soil on the surface; if you put a stick or a spade into it, you come upon the rock a few inches below. On such ground the seed quickly springs, there being no deepness of earth to allow of its spending time in rooting itself. And for the same reason it quickly withers when exposed to the fierce heats which benefit and mature strongly-rooted plants. Precocity and rapid growth are everywhere the forerunners of rapid decay. The oak that is to stand a thousand years does not shoot up like the hop or the creeper. Man whose age is seventy years has a slowly growing infancy and youth, while the insect grows up in a day and dies at night or at the week's end.

The shallow hearer our Lord distinguishes by two characteristics; he *straightway* receives the word, and he receives it *with joy*. The man of deeper character receives the word with deliberation, as one who has many things to take into account and to weigh. He receives it with seriousness, and reverence, and trembling, foreseeing the trials he will be subjected , and he cannot show a light-minded joy. The superficial character responds quickly because there is no depth of inner life. Difficulties which deter men of greater depth do not stagger the superficial. While other men are engaged in giving the word entrance into all the secret places of their life, and are confronting it with their most cherished feelings and ways, that they may clearly see the extent of the changes it will work: while they are pondering it in the majesty of its hope and the vastness of its revelation; while they are striving to forecast all its results in them and upon them; while they are hesitating because they are in earnest, and would receive the word for eternity or not at all, and would give it entrance to the whole of their being, or exclude it altogether,—while others are doing this, the superficial man has settled the whole matter out of hand, and he who yesterday was a known scoffer is to-day a loud-voiced child of the kingdom.

These men may often be mistaken for the most earnest Christians: indeed they are almost certainly taken to be the most earnest; you cannot see the root, and what is seen is shown in greatest luxuriance by the superficial. The earnest man has much of his energy to spend beneath the soil, he cannot show anything till he is sure of the root. He is often working away at the foundation while another is at the copestone. But the test comes. The very influences which exercise and mature the well-rooted character, wither the superficially rooted. The same shallowness of nature which made them susceptible to the gospel and quickly responsive, makes them susceptible to pain, suffering, hardship, and easily defeated. It is so in all departments of life. The superficial are taken with every new thing. The boy is delighted with a new study or a new game, but becomes proficient in neither. The youth is charmed with volunteering, but one season of early rising is more than he can stand: or he is fascinated with the idea that history is an extremely profitable kind of reading; but you know quite well when he asks for the loan of the first volume of Gibbon or Grote, that he will never come to you for the last. The action of the shallow man is in every case hasty, not based on a carefully considered and resolutely accepted plan: he is charmed with the first appearances, and does not look into the matter, and forecast results and consequences. Accordingly, when consequences have to be faced, he is not prepared and gives way.

But how, then, can the shallow man be saved? Is there no provision in the gospel for those who are born with a thin, poor nature? This question scarcely falls to be answered here, because the parable presents one truth regarding shallow natures, which is verified in thousands of instances. Men do thus deal with the word, and thus make shipwreck of faith, and that is all we have here to do with. But passing beyond the parable, it may be right to say that a man's nature may be deepened by the events, and relationships, and conflicts of life. Indeed, that much deepening of character is constantly effected, you may gather from the fact that while many young persons are shallow, the old persons whom you would characterise as shallow are comparatively few.

3. The third faultiness of soil which causes failure in the crop is what is technically known as *dirt*. The soil is not impenetrable, nor is it shallow; it is deep, good land, but it has not been cleaned — there is seed in it already. Sometimes you see a field of wheat brilliantly coloured throughout with poppies; or a field of oats which it is difficult to cut on account of the dense growth of thistles, and of rank grass. But the soil can only feed a certain amount of vegetation, and every living weed means a choked blade of corn. This is a worse case than the others. No crop can be looked for on a beaten road, not much can be expected from a mere peppering of soil upon rock; but here there is rich, deep, loamy mould, that must be growing something, and would, if cared for, yield a magnificent harvest, and yet there is little or nothing but thorns.

This is a picture of the preoccupied heart of the rich, vigorous nature, capable of understanding, appreciating, and making much of the word of the kingdom, but occupied with so many other interests, that only a small part of its energy is available for giving effect to Christ's ideas. These ideas are not excluded from the thoughts, they are welcomed; the mind is full of intelligent interest in Christian truth, and the heart has a real and profound sympathy with the work of Christ in the world and with His spirit, and yet, after all, little practical good proceeds from the man—Christian principle does not come to much in his case—the life shows little result of a specially Christian kind. The reason is that the man is occupied with a multitude of other views, and projects, and cares, and desires, and the peculiarly Christian seed does not get fair play. It influences him, but it is hindered and mixed up with so many other influences that the result is scarcely discernible. The peculiarity of a good field of wheat is not the density of the vegetation, but that the vegetation is all of one kind, is all wheat. Leave the field to itself, you will in a short time have quite as dense a vegetation, but it will be of a multifarious kind. That the field bears wheat only, is the result of cultivation—not merely of sowing wheat, but of preventing anything else from being sown.

The first care of the diligent farmer is to clean his land.

And as there is generally some one kind of weed to which the soil is congenial, and against which the farmer has to wage a continual war, so our Lord here specifies as specially dangerous to us "the care of this world and the deceitfulness of riches." The care of this world has been called the poor man's species of the deceitfulness of riches, and the deceitfulness of riches a variety of the care of this world. There are poor men who have no anxiety, and rich men who are not misled by their riches either into dependence on their wealth, or desire to make it more. But among rich men and poor men alike you will find some or many who would be left without any subject of thought, and any guiding principle in action, if you took from them anxiety about their own position in life. It is this from which all the fruit they bear springs. Take the actions of a year, the annual outcome or harvest of the man, and how much of what he has produced you can trace to this seed—to a mere anxiety about income and position. This is really the seed, this is all that is required to account for a large part of many men's actions.

Our Lord therefore warns us that if the word is to do its work in us, and produce all the good it is meant to produce, it must have the field to itself. It will not do merely to give attention to the word while it is preached: the mind may be clean on the surface, while there remain great knots of roots below, which will inevitably spring up, and by their more inveterate growth choke the word. This is the mistake of many. It is proper, they know, to hear the word—proper to give it fair play. They do make an effort to banish worldly and anxious thoughts, and to give their attention to divine things, but even though they succeed in putting aside for the time distracting thoughts, what of that if they have not the care of the world up by the roots? Cutting down won't do: still less, a mere holding aside of the thorns till the seed be sown. What chance has the seed in a heart from which these eager thoughts and hopes are merely held back for the hour? The cares of the world will just swing over again and meet above the good seed, and shut out the day and every maturing influence. You receive to-day good impressions, you give the good seed entrance, and it begins to spring in you, it prompts you to a reasonable generosity and self-denial. To-morrow morning the tender blade of a desire to purify and prepare your spirit by some real and devout converse with God has sprung up in you, but the habitual craving to be at your work and lose no moment from business crushes and chokes the little blade, and it can no more lift its head. Or the seed has produced even the green ear of a growing habit of living under God's eye, of walking with God and bringing all your transactions before His judgment,—mature fruit seems on the point of being produced by you, when suddenly the promise of a rich harvest is choked by the old coarse thorn of a fondness for rapid profits, which leads you to ambiguous language, and reservations, and unfair dealings, such as you feel separate you from God, and dash your spiritual ardour, and make you feel like a fool and a knave both, when you speak of your citizenship being in heaven. It is vain, then, to hope for the only right harvest of a human life if your heart is sown with worldly ambitions, a greedy hasting to be rich, an undue love of comfort, a true earthliness of spirit. One seed only must be sown in you, and it will produce all needed diligence in business, as well as all fervour of spirit.

These, then, are the three faulty soils to which our Lord chiefly ascribes the failure of the sowing. The question arises, Does the result follow in the moral sowing and in the world of men as uniformly and inevitably as it follows in the sowing of corn in nature? In nature some soils are irreclaimable, vast tracts of the earth's surface are as useless as the sea for the purposes of growing grain. They may indirectly contribute to the fruitfulness of corn lands by influencing the climate, but no one thinks of cultivating these tracts themselves, of sowing the sands of Sahara or the ice-fields of Siberia. But the gospel is to be preached to every creature, because in man there is one important distinction from material nature; he is possessed of free will, of the power of checking to some extent natural tendencies, and preventing natural consequences. Accordingly, we cannot just accept the bare teaching of the parable as the whole truth regarding the operation of the gospel in man's heart, but only as one part of the truth, and that a most important part. The parable enters into no consideration nor explanation of how men arrive at the spiritual conditions here enumerated; but, given those conditions—and they are certainly common however arrived at—given those conditions, the result is failure of the gospel.

In contrast, then, to these three faults of impenetrability, shallowness, and dirt, we may be expected to do something towards bringing to the hearing of the word a soft, deep, clean soil of heart, or, as Luke calls it, "an honest and good heart." There are differences in the crop even among those who bring good hearts; one bears thirty-fold, one sixty, one an hundred-fold. One man has natural advantages, opportunities of position, and so forth, which make his yield greater. One man may have had a larger proportion of seed; in his early days and all through his life he may have been in contact with the word, and in favouring circumstances. But wherever the word is received, and held fast, and patiently cared for, there the life will produce all that God cares to have from it.

Honesty is a prime requisite in hearing the word, and a rare one. Men listen honestly to a lecture on science or history, from which they expect information; but where conduct is aimed at, or a vote is concerned, men commonly listen with minds already made up. It is notorious that men vote as they meant to vote, no matter what is said. If a Liberal were found voting with Conservatives on any important point, some mistake would be supposed. The last thing thought of would be that his convictions had been altered by the speaking. But if we are to hear the word as we ought, we must bring an honest heart, we must not listen with a mind already made up against the gospel, with no intention whatever of being persuaded, cherishing purposes and habits, alongside of which it is impossible the word should grow. On the contrary, we should consider that this is the seed proper to the human heart, and which can alone produce what human life should produce—the word of God, which we must listen to gratefully, humbly, sincerely, greedily, and with the firm purpose of giving it unlimited scope within us. But where is the attentive, painstaking scrutiny of the heart which this demands? Where is the careful husbandry of our souls, which would secure a kindly reception for the word? Where is the jealous challenging of every sentiment, habit, influence, association, that begs for a lodging within us? For where this is, and not elsewhere, we may expect the fruit of the kingdom.

But even this is not enough. The fruitful hearer must not only bring an honest and good heart, he must _keep_ the word. The farmer's work is not finished when he has prepared the soil and sown the seed. If pains be not taken after the sowing, the seed that has fallen on good soil may be taken away as utterly as that which has fallen on the beaten path. The birds scatter over the whole field. We must therefore set a watcher; we must send the harrow over to cover in the seed, and the roller to give the plant a better hold on the soil. The word must not be allowed to take its chance, once it has been heard. Mere hearing does not secure fruit; it goes for nothing. Your labour is lost unless your mind goes back upon what you hear, and you see that it gets hold of you.

All of us have already heard all that is necessary for life and godliness; it remains that we make it our own, that it secure a living root and place in us and in our life. In order to this we must keep the truth; we must bear it in mind, so that whatever else comes before the mind throws new light on it, and gives it a further hold upon us. We must not let the events of the world and the occurrences of our day thrust it from our minds, but must confront it with these, and test it by these, so that thus it may become more real to us, and have a vital influence. One truth received thus, brings forth more fruit than all truth merely understood. It is not the amount of knowledge you have, but the use you put it to—it is not the number of good sayings you have heard and can repeat, that will profit you, but the place in your hearts you have given them, and the connection they have with the motives, and principles, and ruling ideas of your life.

And, therefore, meditation has always been, and must always be, reckoned among the most indispensable means of grace. Since ever saints were, their saintliness has been in great part due to a habit of meditation. Without it, the other means of grace remain helplessly outside of us. The word does not profit except the mind be actively appropriating God's message and revolving it. Prayer is but a deluding form, that means nothing, expects nothing, and receives nothing, if meditation has not provided its material. Unless a man think upon his life and try his ways, his confession can but remove the scum from the surface, leaving the heart burdened and polluted; for the graver sins do not float, but sink deep, and must be dragged for with patience and skill, if not descried through a very rare natural clearness and simplicity of character. It is in the stillness and quiet of our hours of reflection, when the gusts of worldly engagements and desires have died down, that the seeds of grace are deposited in our souls. It is then that our thoughts are free to recognise reasons of humility and causes of thankfulness. It is then that the thought of God resumes its place in our souls, and that the unseen world reasserts its hold upon us. It is then only that the soul, taking a deliberate survey of its own matters, can discover its position and necessities, can assert its claims and determine its future, can begin the knowledge of all things by knowing itself. So that, "if there is a person, of whatever age, or class, or station, who will not be thoughtful, who will not seriously and honestly consider, there *is* no doing him any good."

But there is probably no religious duty so distasteful as meditation to persons whose habits are formed in a state of society like our own. We are, for the most part, infected by the hastiness and overdone activity of the business world. The rapidity and exactness of mechanical action rule and regulate all our personal movements. We are learning to value only what gives us speedily and uniformly achieved and easily appreciated results. We are civilized so nearly to one common level, and are in possession of so many advantages which hitherto have been the monopoly of one class, that competition is keener than ever before; and all our time and energy are demanded for the one purpose of holding our own in things secular. But the dissatisfaction with slow processes, and the desire to get a great deal through our hands, must be checked when we come to the work of meditation. There are processes in nature which you can't hurry. You must let your milk *stand*, if you wish cream. And meditation is a process of mind whose necessary element is the absence of hurry. We must let the mind settle and discharge itself of all irritating distractions and fevering remembrances or hopes; we must reduce it to an equable state, from which it can look out dispassionately upon things, and no longer see the one engrossing object, but all that concerns us in due proportion and real position. The soul must learn to turn a deaf ear to the importunate requirements of the daily life, and turn leisurely and with an unpreoccupied mind to God. Were it only to keep the world at bay, and teach the things of it their subordinate place, these meditative pauses of the soul were of the richest use.

A third and last requisite for the fructification of the seed is, according to Luke, patience. The husbandman does not expect to reap tomorrow what he sowed to-day. He does not incontinently plough up his field again, and sow another crop, if he does not at once see the ripe corn. He watches and waits, and through much that is disappointing and unpromising, nurses his plants to fruitfulness. We also must learn with patience to bring forth fruit; not despairing because we cannot at once do all we would; not sinking under the hardships, sacrifices, failures, sorrows, through which we must win our growth to true fruit-bearing, but animating and cheering our spirits with the sure hope that the seed we have received is vital, and will enable us to produce at last the sound and ripe fruit our lives were meant to yield. We must have patience both to endure all the privations, all the schooling, all the trial of various kinds which may be needful to bring the seed of righteousness to maturity; and also to go on zealously yielding the perhaps despised fruits which are alone possible to us now, and striving always to strike our roots deeper and deeper into the true life.

II.
THE TARES.

"*Another parable put he forth unto them, saying, The kingdom of heaven is likened unto a man which sowed good seed in his field: but while men slept, his enemy came and sowed tares among the wheat, and went his way. But when the blade was sprung up, and brought forth fruit, then appeared the tares also. So the servants of the householder came and said unto him, Sir, didst not thou sow good seed in thy field? from whence then hath it tares? He said unto them, An enemy hath done this. The servants said unto him, Wilt thou then that we go and gather them up? But he said, Nay; lest while ye gather up the tares, ye root up also the wheat with them. Let both grow together until the harvest: and in the time of harvest I will say to the reapers, Gather ye together first the tares, and bind them in bundles to burn them: but gather the wheat into my barn.*" ...

"*Then Jesus sent the multitude away, and went into the house: and his disciples came unto him, saying, Declare unto us the parable of the tares of the field. He answered and said unto them, He that soweth the good seed is the Son of man; the field is the world; the good seed are the children of the kingdom; but the tares are the children of the wicked one; the enemy that sowed them is the devil; the harvest is the end of the world; and the reapers are the angels. As therefore the tares are gathered and burned in the fire; so shall it be in the end of this world. The Son of man shall send forth his angels, and they shall gather out of his kingdom all things that offend, and them which do iniquity; and shall cast them into a furnace of fire: there shall be wailing and gnashing of teeth. Then shall the righteous shine forth as the sun in the kingdom of their Father. Who hath ears to hear, let him hear.*"—MATT. xiii. 24-30; 36-43.

THE TARES.

MATT. xiii. 24-30, 36-43.

IN this parable Christ warns His servants against expecting to see in this world that unmixedly good condition of society which will at length be brought about in the world to come. The kingdom of heaven is to have universal sway, it is to stand without rival and without mixture of evil, but the time is not yet. Those who are themselves within this kingdom must beware of acting as if the final judgment were already passed.

At all times those who believe in God have been perplexed by the fact that this world is so far from a condition of unmingled good. Is it not God's world? He could not sow bad seed. Whence then the tares? Sometimes this has pressed very heavily on the faith of men. It seems so unaccountable a thing that the field of God should not produce an unexceptionable harvest. We believe that God created the world, and created it for a purpose, and originated whatever was needful for the accomplishment of this purpose. Whatever has proceeded from Him can have been only good. No degenerate or noxious grain can have escaped His hand. And yet, look at the result. How difficult in some parts of the field to see any fruit of God's sowing; how mixed everywhere is the evidence that this is God's field. Is it not the ill-cultivated patch of a careless proprietor, or the ill-conditioned, unworkable tract on which the wealthy owner has not wasted the labour which might better be expended elsewhere? Has God mistaken the capabilities of His field, or does He not care to develope them? or does He like this mingled crop? Does He not sympathise with His servants when they grieve over this sad waste? Has murder a horror only for us? does falsehood excite no indignation but in us? are violence and lust, disease and wretchedness matters of indifference to God? What do we see in the world? Centuries of folly, passion, toil, and anguish; countries desolated by the vices of their inhabitants; diseases which the most skilful cannot alleviate, nor the most callous view without a shudder; sorrow and sin more bitter, more cruel, more appalling than any disease. And this is the lot of God; here He delights to dwell. On no field of all His possessions has He spent more. Well may we join with the servants and say, "Sir, didst not Thou sow good seed in Thy field? From whence then hath it tares?"

But Christ comes and inaugurates a new order of things, and all evil will disappear from earth. Man's natural condition is but the dark back-ground on which the saving grace of God may display its brilliant effects. God Himself comes and dwells with men, rolling back the heavy darkness with the light of His presence and wisdom, infusing His own life into all. Now will the earth yield her increase. Alas! the failure of the harvest of God is in many respects even more conspicuous in the Church of Christ than in the non-Christian world. The very method adopted to redeem the failure of the original creation seems itself also to be in great part failure. We are perplexed when we find wild and useless vegetation in the outlying wilderness, but when we enter the garden of God, and within that redeemed enclosure still find weeds and disorder, our perplexity deepens into dismay. Yet the fact is that, with scarcely an exception, all the useless and pernicious plants found outside Christendom are found also within. Where is there to be found a more passionate greed of gain, or a more self-indulgent luxury, or a more thorough-going wordliness than among the masses of the trading Christian races? The gambling, the unscrupulous hasting to be rich, the cruel and heart-hardening selfishness that abound in our own society are only made more deceptive and dangerous by being crossed with plants of heavenly origin, and by disguising their true nature under the flowers of Christian utterances, occasional charities, seeming repentances, and ineffective purposing of better things. Lust and villainy, fraud, malice, cruelty, — these noxious plants flourish within as without the Christian pale. And it is within Christendom we must look, if we would see some of the worst species of human iniquity. One is ashamed to read the history of the Church. Beside the good corn whose full ear bends in humble maturity of service, the deadly plant of delusive self-righteousness rears its pretentious and empty head. Ignorance, fear, and self-seeking have imitated every Christian grace, till the whole ground is covered with an overgrowth that hides from the eye the healthy plants of Christ's own sowing. Insincerity, superstition, obscurantism, intolerance, pious fraud, the prostitution of the highest interests of men to aims the most contemptible and vile, the disguising of a rotten character under a professed faith and hope of the most elevating and glorious kind,—these are the plants which flourish in the garden of God. All that is double, all that is mean, all that is craven, all that is shallow and earthly in human nature, seems to be stimulated by this cultivated soil. The field which was to be the nursery of free souls who, with eyes unscaled to see the true beauty of eternal goodness, should devote themselves with courage and generosity to the common good, has become a paddock in which the timorous seek refuge from a future they dread, and in which every low desire thinks it may burrow with impunity. Looking at Christendom as it actually is, we may well ask, Is this what Christ sowed? Is this what He has produced on earth? Is this the kind of Christendom He intended? "Sir, did'st not Thou sow good seed in Thy field? From whence then hath it tares?"

The explanation of this disappointing state of matters is given in the words, "An enemy hath done this." It is not the result of Christianity, but of agencies opposed to Christianity. To sow a neighbour's field with noxious seed is in some countries a common device for venting spite or wreaking vengeance; and a more villainous injury can scarcely be imagined. It blasts hope; it is a long grievance, daily meeting the eye and wearing out the spirit till the harvest; it spoils the crop and injures the soil. It seems to say that all this time, from day to day, I have an enemy who hates me, so that there can be no truer joy to him than that which gives me sorrow. He cannot be happy if I am. My happiness is his misery; my misery his greatest happiness. This is his spirit, the spirit of the Evil One, by whomsoever shown; a spirit not wholly absent from our relations with other men, but betrayed even when we suppose ourselves to be animated with righteous indignation or warrantable revenge.

There is something characteristically devilish too, in the deed being done "when men slept;" when the sun has gone down and the wrath of man begins to quiet and cool; when men of right mind are resolving not to act in heat, or be provoked to unworthy and low-toned iniquities, but to think over their matters; when they are perhaps dreaming that they are once again boys together, and walking folded in one another's arms; when the stillness and solemn grandeur of night rebuke the loud clamour and petty wranglings of men; when, at least, a pause is given to sin, this spirit's malignity tires not, but like the beasts of prey is roused to a livelier activity, and recognizes the darkness and quiet as his peculiar season. In him there is no folding of his hands from evil, no wearying, no hesitation in his course, no questioning whether, after all, this is not too bad, no desire to mingle with it a little good, no desire of rest or forgetfulness, but the grateful memory of past wickedness inciting him to new iniquities.

Such being the state of the field, and such its cause, what are the servants to do? "Wilt Thou that we go and gather out these tares?"

Men are ever for prompt measures. "Lord, wilt Thou that we command fire to come down from heaven and consume them?" Few understand the sparing of profligate cities for the sake of ten righteous men. We inwardly grudge that there should be so little difference now manifested between God's treatment of the righteous and the wicked; and that it should only at intervals appear that the former are His peculiar possession. Did our feelings rule the world, we should allow very few tares to appear. We cannot wait, but must anticipate the harvest. This and that other effective propagator of falsehood, would it not be well if he were out of the way? Would not good men come to a quicker and more fruitful maturity, were they not continually damaged by the blighting influences of sceptical literature, worldly society, superficial religionists?

"Let both grow together until the harvest," is the law of the Master. Again and again the Church has, in the face of this parable, taken upon her to root out infidels and heretics. The reasoning has been summary: We are Christ's, these men are Satan's, let us destroy them. All such attempts violently to hasten the consummation, and to make the field of the world appear uniform, have most disastrously hindered the growth of true religion. The servants have wrought a more frightful desolation and barrenness in the field than anything which could have resulted from the existence of the tares.

It is, indeed, not always easy to know how far we should act upon the acknowledged fact of a man's ungodliness. In this country there is a strong feeling against opinions which are believed to be dangerous; perhaps it may be said that the animosity excited by a man's profession of atheism is more vehement and active than that which immorality excites. And though, happily, we do not now go so far as to remove such persons from the world, we do not scruple to visit them with serious social and civil disabilities. Now this parable emits the law regarding such persons. It does not say the world is as it ought to be; it does not say there is no distinction, or a very insignificant one, between good and bad men, or between Christians and atheists; but it enjoins upon us the necessity of refraining from acting upon this distinction to the injury of any. Punishments must be inflicted by society on its injurious members, but not on the score of their ungodliness or unprofitableness in Christ's kingdom. The distinction between a criminal and a benefactor of his country may not be so great as between a ripe Christian and a full-blown atheist; but while we are compelled to act upon the former distinction, and pluck up the criminal from his place, and banish him from our society, the latter distinction is not fully manifested, and must not be fully acted upon in this world. The man who habitually swears, or leads a grossly immoral life, or propagates infidelity, may do a great deal more harm than the starving boy who steals a loaf; but we are called upon to punish the latter and not the former. And in so far as we damage the prospects, or asperse the good name, of any man because we consider him "tares," and not wheat, in so far we fly in the face of this parable.

The reasonableness of this method of delay is sufficiently obvious. Within the Church itself it is often impossible even to be as sure as the servants of the parable were that there is darnel sown among the wheat, or at least to discriminate between the wheat and the darnel. An opinion, or a practice, which is at first sight condemned as scandalous or full of danger, may turn out to be sound and wholesome. But if no time be allowed it to grow, if it be summarily pronounced tares, and thrown over the hedge, the good fruit it might have borne is thrown away with it. Truth may be in the minority—always is at first in the minority; and if, as the servants view the field, they merely take a vote as to what is wholesome and what poisonous, they are likely enough to do evil rather than good.

And even where it is certain that evil has sprung up in the Church, it is a further question whether it should be summarily removed. This parable, it is true, is not the guide for the action of the rulers of the Church towards its members; but, indirectly, a warning against hasty action is given to those in authority. False doctrine may sometimes be more easily got rid of, if it be regarded in silence, or with a few words of convincing exposure, than if it be signalized with assault. No man who had any regard for his field would carry a seeding thistle through every part of it, and give it a shake in every corner.

But our Lord Himself in the parable assigns two reasons for this abstinence from immediate action. First, you are not to root up tares, because you will inevitably root up good corn with them. It is almost impossible to pull up a single stalk of corn by the root; you may break it off, but if you take up its root you are almost sure to bring away with it a number of other stalks and a mass of soil. The one root refuses to be detached from the rest—a striking representation of what happens when injury is inflicted on any member of society. You cannot injure one man, and one only. In him you strike his children, his friends, his followers if he be a man of influence. No man is so forlorn that none will be made lonelier by his death, or be embittered or saddened by his misfortune. We live for the most part in little circles, bound one to the other by indissoluble relationships, nurtured from one soil, and matured by common interests and feelings. And these circles are not separate from one another, but some member of your circle belongs also to another; and so the whole world is linked together, and you cannot put forth your hand and strike any man whose pain shall not be felt by others, nor thrust him from you without repelling all who are attached to him. And of those who are attached to him, are you sure there are none who belong to the kingdom, no little blade springing up by his root, which, did you let it grow, would abound in fruit? For, that a man is evil himself, is no proof that all his connections are evil. On the contrary, an ungodly man will often cling to those who belong to the kingdom, as if somehow they must find entrance for him along with themselves. A father who cannot change his own ways nor yield the opinions of his youth, seeks to protect his children from the influences that destroyed himself, and to atone for his own barrenness by their productiveness. Some who are held as by a terrible fatality from winning the kingdom, will yet entreat others to use violence to enter it. Even the most profligate have commonly some one ripe and living soul devoted to them, who could wish that himself were accursed for their kinsmen according to the flesh.

But this first reason rests upon the second: and that is, that the time is coming when the distinction between the wheat and the tares is to be acted upon. Only let a man accept the account here given of the end of the tares, and he will have very little desire to anticipate or hasten that end. When God says, "Vengeance is mine, I will repay," we feel that the darkest injustice and wrong-doing will be adequately taken account of. When we reflect that what has roused our indignation has also been observed by God, and will be dealt with by Him, not only is our indignation mitigated, but, in view of the judgment of God, our pity is moved towards the transgressor. We were about to punish as if we were the offended party, as if we saw the matter in all its bearings and could justly judge it, and as if we had the right punishment at hand; but when this final judgment looms in sight we see how different are God's judgments and God's punishments from ours, and an awful pity possesses us. Believe that the bar of God lies across the path of each of us, believe that a veritable sifting of men is to be, and that all men are to be allotted to suitable destinies, and compassion will extinguish every other feeling you may have cherished towards the wicked. The position in which we in this life are is full of awe, and fitted also to engender in us the tenderest feelings one towards another—growing up as we are side by side, but with destinies perhaps immeasurably wide asunder; here for a little united root to root, and yet, it may be, severed to all eternity. Could any position be better calculated to banish from our minds all indifference to one another's prospects, all sullen and revengeful feelings, all variance and hatred, and to quicken within us a true affection and compassion, a considerate and helpful tenderness?

The bearing of this parable, then, on ourselves cannot be mistaken. Wheat and darnel, it says, are almost identical in appearance, and are, in the meantime, treated as if the one was as valuable as the other; but let them grow, and the fruit will prove that the root principle of the one is different as possible from the other; the one is good food, the other poison. And they will eventually be treated accordingly. Everything must ultimately find its place according to its nature; not according to its appearance, nor according to any pretensions put forward in its behalf, but only and simply according to its own real character and quality. Each of us is growing *to* something, and from some root. No one may be able to say—perhaps you yourself are unable to say—to which kind and to what root you belong; perhaps you cannot confidently affirm what it is to which you are growing, but beneath all appearances there is in you a real character, a root that determines what you shall grow to. As we grow up in society together, one man is in the main very like another. Of two of your friends, it may be the one who makes least profession of religion that you would go to in a difficulty in which much generous help and toil are needed. Take a regiment of soldiers or a ship's crew, and you may find the ungodly as brave and self-sacrificing in action, as observant of discipline as the others. There may be little to show that there is a radical difference in character; sometimes, of course, this difference is very rapidly manifested, but in general there is so much similarity as to make it notorious that the Church is not distinctly marked off from the world. Society does resemble a field in which the wheat and the darnel are still in the blade, and can be discriminated only by a very careful observer.

So that, first, this is apt to make the darnel think itself as good as the wheat. If we merely look at appearances we are apt to think that, take us all round, there is not much to choose between the wheat and us. We see in truly

Christian people evil tempers, a revengeful, tyrannical, ungenerous spirit, we detect bitterness and meanness in them, sometimes sensuality, and a keen eye for worldly advantage, and we are encouraged to believe that really we stand comparison with them very favourably. So no doubt you do. The world would be insufferable if all men had the spirit which many Christians show. But that is not the point. The question is not whether you are not at present, to all appearance, as useful and pleasant a member of society as they; but the question is, whether there is not that in them which will grow to good, and whether there is not that in you which will grow to evil. Do you, that is to say, sufficiently consider this parable, which most frankly admits that at present, so far as things have yet grown, there may be no very marked difference between the children of the kingdom and others, but at the same time emphatically declares that the root is different, and that, therefore, the life is really of a different quality, and will in the long run *appear* to be different? The question is, what is your root? What is it that is producing the actual life you are making, and the actual character you are growing into? What is the motive power? Is it mere desire to get on, or craving for a good position among men? Is it respect for your own good name? or are you a child of the kingdom? Are you the result of the word of the kingdom? that is, is your conduct being more and more animated and regulated, and is your character being more and more formed, by the belief that God calls you to live for Him and for eternity? Do you like this world really better than one in which you have a hope only of spiritual joys, of true fellowship with God, and holiness of heart? Can you make good to your own mind, that in some quite intelligible sense you are rooted in Christ, and grow out of Him? It is the root you live from which will eventually show itself in you, and determine your eternal position.

Again, the urgency of the call to Christ is deadened by the fact that we are not *treated* differently at present. Men argue: we get on well enough now, and the future will take care of itself. But this is to brush aside at a blow all that we are told of the connection of the present with the future. This state bears to a coming world the relation which seed-time bears to harvest. No violence will be done to you at present to convince you that you are useless to God. No judgment will be declared, no punishment inflicted — that were out of season, for in this life we are left to choose freely and without compulsion, whether we desire to be in God's kingdom or not. In this life you must judge yourself and do violence to yourself. But this argues nothing regarding the future life. It is only then a beginning is made of treatment corresponding to character.

Lastly, not only is the darnel apt to think itself as good as the wheat, but the wheat is apt to think itself no better than the darnel. You can never outstrip others in good as you would like. You are troubled because they seem to be as regular, as zealous, as successful in duty as you. Possibly, too, they are not only as judicious in conduct, as generous, as true, of as good report as yourselves, but, moreover, exercise a healthier influence than you do on those they live with. Some natural infirmity of temper has fixed its indelible brand on you, something which makes you less attractive and less influential than you might otherwise be. Or perhaps you are choked by uncongenial surroundings, kept down in growth by the tares around you, often betrayed into sins which better company would have made impossible. Are you somehow continually kept back from growing to all you feel you might grow to? Is there good in you that has never yet been elicited? Look then to the end, when "the righteous shall shine forth as the sun in the kingdom of their Father." Be sure only that there is that in you which will shine forth if the hindrances and blinds are removed. There is no change to pass on the wheat; but only the tares shall be taken away, and it will stand revealed, good corn. Bring forth your fruit in patience: maintain the real distinction between good and evil, and at last it will be apparent.

III.

THE MUSTARD SEED.

"*Another parable put he forth unto them, saying, The kingdom of heaven is like to a grain of mustard seed, which a man took, and sowed in his field: which indeed is the least of all seeds: but when it is grown, it is the greatest among herbs, and becometh a tree, so that the birds of the air come and lodge in the branches thereof.*"—MATT. xiii. 31, 32.

THE MUSTARD SEED.

MATT. xiii. 31, 32.

NEITHER the parable of the Sower nor the parable of the Tares was calculated to elate those who were interested in the kingdom of heaven. The hindrances and disappointments incident to the establishment of that kingdom were too plainly stated to be gratifying. It was not exhilarating to the hearers of these parables to learn that the state of things to which they had eagerly looked forward as the realization of their ideal, and the embodiment of all excellence, could not be actually achieved on earth. In this parable of the mustard seed our Lord turns the other side of the picture, and affirms that the little movement already stirring society would grow to vast dimensions; that the influences He was introducing so unobtrusively into human history were vital, and would one day command attention and be productive of untold good. He does not anticipate the parable of the leaven, and explain the precise mode of the spread of Christianity, but merely predicts the fact of its growth. He invites us to compare the visible cause with the visible result; He directs our thoughts to the two facts of the small beginning and the ultimate grandeur of the kingdom of heaven, and suggests that the reason of this growth is that the originating principle of the kingdom has vitality in it.

It is the study of the laws of growth which, in recent years, has given so great an impulse to human knowledge and to the delight men find in nature. How this world has come to be what it is; its rude and unpromising beginnings, and its steady progress towards perfection; the development of an infinitely various and complicated life from a few rudimentary forms;—these have been the commonest subjects of scientific investigation. It has been shown that everything we are ourselves now connected with has grown out of something which went before; that nothing is self-originated. The growth of languages and religions, of customs and forms of government, of races and nations, has been traced; and a new interest has thus been imparted to all things, for everything is found to have a history which carries us back to the most unlikely roots, and is full of surprises. Creation excites wonder; but growth excites an intelligent admiration and wonder as well. For, after all investigation and exposition of its laws, growth remains marvellous. That the swift-flying bird, sensitive to the remotest atmospheric changes, should grow out of the motionless, strictly encased egg, is always an astonishment. That the wide-branching tree, hiding the sky with its foliage, should be the product of a small, insignificantly shaped seed, never ceases to excite wonder. Nothing could well be more unlike the bird than the egg; nothing less like a tree than the seed it has grown out of; but by an unseen and ultimately inscrutable force the egg becomes a bird, and the seed grows into a tree. To see the stateliest pile of building filling the space which before was empty, makes on appeal to the imagination: that kind of increase we seem to understand; stone is added to stone by the will and toil of man. But when we look at the deeply-rooted and wide-branching tree, and think of the tiny seed from which all this sprang without human will or toil, but by an internal vitality of its own, we are confronted by the most mysterious and fascinating of all things, the life that lies unseen in nature.

In the difference, then, between the beginning and the maturity of our Lord's kingdom there was nothing exceptional. The same difference may be observed in the case of almost every person or influence that has greatly helped mankind. Many of the inventions to which we are hourly indebted entered the world like little seeds casually blown to their resting-place; they floated on, unheeded, unobserved, till at last, apparently by the merest chance, they caught somewhere, and became productive. It is the very commonness of this career, from small to great, to which our Lord appeals for the encouragement of His disciples. Here is the least among seeds; it flies before your breath; it is not noticed in the balance; a miser would scarce trouble himself to blow it from the scale; the hungry bird will not pause in his flight to pick it up; but let a few years go by, and that seed shall have become a tree, in which the birds of the air may lodge, and which no force can uproot. The seed, as you now see it, is doing and can do nothing that the tree does; it casts no shade, it shelters no birds, it yields no fruit or timber, it does not fill the eye and complete the landscape; but give it time, and it will do all these things, as nothing else will or can.

In this parable, then, our Lord gave expression to three of the ideas which frequently recurred to His mind regarding the kingdom of heaven: —1st. Its present apparent insignificance; 2d. Its vitality; 3d. Its future grandeur.

1. Our Lord recognized that to the uninstructed, ordinary observer His kingdom must in its origin appear insignificant, "the least of all seeds." It might seem less likely to prevail,

and to become a universal benefit, than some other contemporary systems or influences. In point of fact, so extravagant did Christ's claim to be a benefactor of the race appear, that those who wished to mock Him could devise no more telling and bitter taunt than to bow before Him and salute Him as a king. That such a tame-spirited, forsaken person should attain a place among the strong-handed rulers of the world seemed altogether too preposterous. The Roman magistrate, before whom He was arraigned on the charge of rebellion against Cæsar, found it difficult to treat the charge seriously. Open the histories of His time, and your eyes are dazzled with the magnificence of other monarchs, and the magnitude of their works, but He is barely named—so little known, that He is sometimes misnamed through sheer ignorance. It was no discredit to the most learned and accurate of historians to know nothing of Jesus Christ. This obscurity and insignificance would not have been disconcerting to the followers of a mere teacher, for the best teaching is rarely appreciated in the first generation; but as our Lord claimed to be a lawgiver and real king, it certainly did not bode well for His kingdom that during His life-time so few obeyed or even knew Him.

The very circumstance that He was a Jew might have seemed to those of His contemporaries who were best able to judge, enough in itself to ensure the defeat of any purpose of universal sway. The exclusive character of the religious and social ideas of the Jew, and the hostility with which this exclusiveness was returned by other nations, seemed to make it most improbable that all men should be brought into one common brotherhood and community by a Jew. Moreover, Jesus Himself was no Hellenist, whose Jewish ideas might have been modified by Greek learning and cosmopolitan associations and customs; but He was a Jew of purest blood and upbringing, educated in all Jewish customs and ideas, and subjected to the ordinary Jewish influences, never visiting other lands, and rarely speaking to any but His own countrymen. So far as we know, He made no enquiries into the state of other countries, and read no books to inform Himself; He did not send emissaries to Rome, inviting men to consider His claims; He made no overtures of any kind to men at a distance;—that is to say, He did not present Himself as a grown tree branching friendly outwards, to which might flock the birds of the air which had been driven out by the winter of their own land, and had wandered far in search of food, and were weary from their long flight.

Even among His own people, from whom He might have expected a hearty welcome and loyal advocacy, He met with either contemptuous neglect or positive opposition. He obtained no recognized standing, even among the Jews. Those who formed the opinions of society pronounced Him an impostor, and the people were so completely convinced by them, that they clamoured for His death. The few who were attached to Him, and who thoroughly believed in His sincerity and spiritual greatness, persistently misunderstood the essential parts of His purpose and teaching. They could not, even to the last, rid their minds of the natural impression that His being crucified as a malefactor was the end of all their hopes. And is it not probable that even Jesus Himself, as He was ignominiously hurried to His death by a handful of Roman soldiers, may have been tempted to think, What is there in this to regenerate a world? Will such an everyday incident even be remembered next Passover? Certainly, so far as appearances went, and in the judgment of all who saw and were interested, His kingdom was at that time comparable to anything but a firmly-rooted and flourishing tree.

After the resurrection of Christ, His kingdom became slightly more visible, but its prospects must still have seemed extremely doubtful. A handful of men, none of them having much weight in the community, or being in any way remarkable, compose the force which is to conquer the world. To win a single soul to an unpopular cause is difficult, but these men were summoned to the task of converting all nations. They had no ancient institutions, no well-tried methods, no strong associations, no funds, no friends to back them. On the contrary, everything seemed banded against them. Teachers, who disagreed in all else, combined to scorn the folly of the cross; emperors, who would allow every other form of religion, could not tolerate that of Jesus. Everywhere the world was already preoccupied by ancient and jealously-guarded religions, by habits, and ideas, and traditions adverse to the spirit of Christ. The instrument, too, which was to convert the world seemed as powerless as the men who were to wield it. They were to tell of Jesus, of His life, His death, His resurrection. Was it not vain to expect that remote and barbarous races would become so attached to a person they had never seen, that they would govern their passions and amend their lives for His sake? Was it likely that, on the word of unknown men, the person of an unknown man should become the centre of the world, commanding the adherence of all, and imparting to all the most powerful influences?

2. But at the very moment when our Lord was most conscious of the poor figure His

kingdom made in the eyes of men, He was absolutely confident of its final greatness, because, small as it was, *it was of the nature of seed*. It had a vital force in it that nothing could kill; a germinating and expansive power which would only be quickened by opposition. His own death, the obscurity and limitation to which His cause was at first subjected, were not, He knew, the first symptoms of permanent oblivion, but were only the sowing of the seed. He was no more anxious than the farmer is who, for the first week or two, sees no appearance of his plants above ground. Our Lord knew that, could He only get His kingdom accepted at even one small point of earth, the growth would inevitably and in good time follow.

There are certain human qualities, ideas, utterances, and acts which are vital and must grow. They have in them an expansive, living energy; they sink into the hearts and minds of men, and propagate a lasting influence. What, then, is the vital element in Christianity? What is it that has given permanence and growth to the kingdom of Christ? What did Christ plant that no one else has planted? What is it that keeps Him in undying remembrance, and gathers from each new generation fresh subjects for His kingdom? It is not the wisdom and beauty of His teaching. That might have led us to immortalize His words by reprinting and quoting them. Neither is it solely the holiness of His life, or the love He showed. These might have kindled in us admiration, but could never have prompted that real allegiance which is implied in a kingdom. But it is chiefly the revelation of God in Him which draws men to Him. In His death and resurrection we get assurance of Divine love and Divine power abiding in Him. It is God in Him that draws us. We cleave to Him, because through Him we are lifted to God and to eternity. In His brief career He gives us a perception of the reality of the spiritual world, the permanence of the individual, and the nearness and love of God, which nothing else gives us. In Him men meet a God satisfying all their expectations; so devoted to their interests, that He lives and dies with them, and for them; so hopeful regarding them, that He proclaims pardon and newness of life to sinners; so victorious over all the evils weighing upon man, that He conquers death itself, and throws open to all the gates of life everlasting.

The seed is the highest product of the plant: the fruit is but the accompaniment of the seed; it is into the seed that the plant each year puts its life. So in man, the ripest product of the individual, the actions or words into which he gathers up his whole character and strength,— it is these which are vital and germinant. The vital element in the life of Christ cannot be mistaken: it was, in a word, the Divine Son giving Himself for us; God expressing the fulness of Divine sympathy and sacrifice in our behalf—a seed, surely, from which great things must spring.

3. Our Lord points to the eventual greatness of His kingdom. The despised seed, ground into the soil under the heel of contempt and hatred, will become a tree, whose leaves shall be for the healing of the nations. The disciples do not seem to have gathered from this parable the encouragement which was laid up for them in it; but an instructed onlooker might have admonished the crucifiers of the Lord that they were fulfilling His words—"That cross which you are setting up, and which you will take down before the sun is set, shall stand in the thought of countless millions as the point of earth most illuminated by the light of heaven; that blood which you are shedding, as you would pour water out of your way on the ground, is to be recognised by your fellowmen and by God as precious, as that by which the souls of men are redeemed and purified."

The kingdom of heaven has indeed become a tree. It would be difficult to count even the greater branches of it; difficult to number the various twigs which depend upon the central stem; impossible to count the leaves or to form an idea of the fruit which, through past years, has gradually ripened and fallen from it. This religion which emanated from a country so detested by the surrounding nations that they might be expected to say of it, as the Jews themselves of Nazareth, "Can any good thing come out of Judea?"—this religion propagated by Jews who had become Christians, so that being excommunicated by their own countrymen, and naturally hated by all other people, they seemed the most unlikely instruments to commend new ideas; this religion which could offer no high posts or secular rewards, and numbered few wise, wealthy, or noble among its adherents; which would not tolerate other religions, and yet proclaimed doctrines which excited the ridicule of the educated; which demanded from all alike, not only an absolutely pure morality and a repulsive and humbling self-renunciation, but a newness of spirit impossible to the natural man; this religion which seemed to have everything against it, which seemed like a sickly child which it was scarcely worth calling by a name to be remembered as a living thing,—this has grown to be the greatest of all powers for good in the world. The seed determines the character of all that springs from it; the quality of the fruit and its abundance may vary with the nature of the soil and with the presence or absence of careful cultivation and other advantages, but the tree will still be recognisable as of that kind to which the seed belonged. And as the seed of the kingdom of heaven was love and holiness and Divine power, so have similar fruits been borne by men wherever the kingdom has come. The outmost branch, looking in an opposite direction from the distant branches on the other side of the tree, and apparently quite dissociated from these branches, is still identified with them by the fruit it bears. Wherever in all these past ages, and in all the scattered countries of Christendom, there has been a Christ-like life; wherever sinners have been drawn to love God and hate their sin through the knowledge of the cross; wherever in hope of a blessed immortality men have borne the sorrows of time without bitterness, and committed their dead to the grave in expectation of a life beyond,—there the seed Christ sowed has been showing its permanent vitality.

The figure of the tree inevitably suggests other considerations regarding the Church, besides those which are directly taught in the parable. The tree, with its single stem and countless branches, is only too true a picture of the diverging belief and worship of those who own a common root in Christ. Sometimes, indeed, one is tempted to compare the Church to one of those trees in which the branches diverge as soon as they appear above ground, so that you cannot tell whether the tree is really one or many. In some of its aspects, again, the Church resembles the huge tree that stands on the village green, looking benignly down on the joys of the young, and giving shade and shelter to the aged, seeing generation after generation drop away like its own leaves, but itself living through all with the freshness of its early days; its lower bark only marked by the ambition of those who have sought to identify their now scarcely legible names with its undecaying life, but whose work has after all not entered into the life of the tree, but only marred its external hull. Again, we see that some of the lowest, earliest grown branches are quite dead or drooping; that Christianity has passed from the peoples among whom it first found root, and that satyrs dance where the praises of Christ were once sung. It would almost seem as if there were a melancholy accuracy in the figure used in the parable, and that the tree, having once attained its full dimensions, grows no more. After some years the rapid growth which was so striking in the young tree is no longer discernible. It maintains equal or perhaps stronger life, but spring after spring you look in vain for any discernible increase in size. But certain it is that this plant which Christ planted has shown vitality, drawing nutriment from every soil in which it has been tried, and assimilating to its own life and substance all that is good in the soil, using the faculties and accomplishments, the literary or artistic or commercial leanings and gifts of the various races so as to further the true welfare of men; gathering strength from sunshine and storm alike, cherishing a hidden life through the long winters when every branch seemed hopelessly dead, and drawing supplies of vitalizing moisture from sources beyond the ken of man when the scorching heats threatened to wither up every living leaf. The tree is growing now, gradually absorbing into itself all the widening thoughts of men, and by the chemistry of its own life extracting nutriment from criticism, from philosophy, from research, from social and political movements, from everything that forms the great stirring human world in which it is rooted; not afraid to stand out in the open and face the day, but gaining vigour from every brisker air that tosses its branches.

This parable was spoken for the encouragement of the disciples: it is needed still for the encouragement of all who are interested in the extension of Christ's kingdom. In many respects our outlook is even more hopeless than that of the first disciples. The novelty, the first enthusiasm, the external signs, are all gone; the solidarity of the Church is also gone, and in its place we have to overcome the discrediting exhibitions of discord and internal conflict, as well as the weakening influence of scepticism, and the slowly corroding materialism that is destroying the very foundations of religion. The missionary enterprise of the first disciples seems never to have extended very far from the Mediterranean coasts. They were unaware of the vast multitudes beyond, and of the solidity and attractiveness of some of the religions already in occupation; whereas to the eye of the modern Church populations are disclosed, numbered by hundreds of millions, and adhering to religions more ancient and more outwardly impressive than our own. Our zeal, too, is slackened by the very fact that all this yet remains to be done; that Christianity should have been growing for nearly two thousand years, and that it has not yet convinced all men of its superiority, and that in places where it has been most ardently received it has borne fruit of which every man must feel ashamed.

To all persons who are disheartened, whether by the apparent fruitlessness of their own efforts or by the slow growth of the Church at large, this parable says, You must measure things not by their size, but by their vitality. What you can do may be very little, and once it is done there may be no sign of results; but if you put yourself into it, if it come from the heart—a heart whose earnestness and hope are the result of contact with Christ—then fruit will one day be borne. You must have some imagination. You must have some faith that will enable you to wait patiently for fruit. Make sure that what you sow is good seed; that what you teach your children is true; that what you strive to introduce into society is sound and helpful; that the ideas you propagate, the charity you support, the industry you seek to advance, are all such as belong to the kingdom of Christ, and you may be sure your labour is not lost. You may not see the results of your actions. You may not see full grown the trees of your planting, but your children will lie under their shade, and dream of your sheltering forethought, and strive to fulfil your best purposes. Do not be discouraged because all is not yet done on earth, and much remains for you to do; do not be discouraged because there is room for sacrifice and faith, devotedness, and wisdom, and love, and skill. It is not hot-house results we seek to produce, nor, like the Indian jugglers, to make a tree visibly shoot up by sleight of hand. What we look for is the real growth of human good, and this can be accomplished by no rapid and magical processes, but only by the patient nutrition of the soil by all that is truest and deepest in human nature, and by all that is most real and most testing in human effort. Honestly seek the growth of this tree, and be not too greatly dismayed by the portentous difficulties of the task. "He that observeth the wind shall not sow, and he that regardeth the clouds shall not reap. As thou knowest not what is the way of the spirit, even so thou knowest not the works of God who maketh all. In the morning sow thy seed, and in the evening withhold not thy hand, for thou knowest not whether shall prosper, either this or that, or whether they both shall be alike good."

In conclusion, is it not relevant to ask whether we have joined the Christian Church, because it is large, or because it is living? Simon in the temple held all Christendom in his arms, and yet felt sure the redemption of the world was nigh. Is your faith like his? Is it the Person of Christ and not what has grown round His person that you cleave to? Do you find *that* in Christ which compels you to say that, though you were the only Christian, yourself the Church visible, you must abide by Him? Is there some independence in your choice, some individuality in your experience? Can you say, with some significance, "I know Him in whom I have believed"? or do you but adopt the fashion that prevails, and feel the propriety and safety of going with the majority? In any case it is well that you recognise that there is this tree planted by the Lord Himself, and still growing upon earth. There is upon earth a society of men not always easy to find, but in true sympathy with Him ; a progress of human affairs to which He gave the initial impulse. There is on earth a tree, the seed of which is His own life, whose growing bulk embodies, from generation to generation, all that exists in the world of His purpose and work. The good He intended for men He deposited in that seed. He came to impart to men permanent blessings. He saw our condition, recognised what we needed, and introduced into the world what He knew would achieve the happiness of every one of us.

IV.
THE LEAVEN.

"*Another parable spake he unto them: The kingdom of heaven is like unto leaven, which a woman took, and hid in three measures of meal, till the whole was leavened.*"—MATT. xiii. 33.

THE LEAVEN.

MATT. xiii. 33.

THIS parable directs attention to two points connected with the spread of Christianity. It illustrates—

1. First, the *kind* of change which Christianity works in the world; and

2. Second, the *method* by which this change is wrought.

1. First, our Lord here teaches that the change which He meant to effect in the world was a change, not so much of the outward form, as of the spirit and character of all things. The propagation of His influence is illustrated not by the figure of a woman taking a mass of dough and baking it up into new loaves of a shape hitherto unseen; but by the figure of a woman putting that into the dough which alters the character of the whole mass. She may set on the table loaves that are to all appearance the same as the old, but no one will taste them without perceiving the difference. The old shapes are retained, the familiar marks appear still on the loaves, but it is a

different bread. The appearance remains the same, the reality is altered. The form is retained, but the character is changed.

There are two ways in which you may revolutionize any country or society. You may either pull down all the old forms of government, or you may fill them with men of a different spirit. If an empire is going to ruin, you may either change the empire into a republic, or you may put the right man in the office of emperor. If any society or club or association has become effete and a nuisance, doing harm instead of good, you may reform it either by revising its constitution, making new laws and regulations, and so making it a new society, or you may fill its official positions with men of a right spirit, leaving its form of constitution untouched. A watch stops, and somebody tells you it needs new works, but the watchmaker tells you it only needs cleaning. A machine refuses to work, and people think the construction is wrong, but the skilled mechanic pushes aside the ignorant crowd and puts all to rights with a few drops of oil. "Your bread is unwholesome," says the public to the baker, and he says, "Well, I'll send you loaves of a new shape;" but the woman of the parable follows the wiser course of altering the quality of the bread.

Few distinctions are of wider application, few need more careful pondering by all of us whether in our social, political, or religious capacity. Many of us take a huge interest in the institutions of our country, and are ready to lay our finger on this and that as needing reform. This parable should therefore haunt the ear, and always suggest the question: Is this or that institution radically bad? or, supposing good and wise men were working it, would it not serve a good purpose? What is wanted in the world is not new forms, but a new spirit in the present forms. New forms, new institutions, new regulations, new occupations, new trades, new ways of occupying our time, new customs are really as little to the purpose as putting the old make of bread into new shapes. What our Lord by this parable warns us to aim at and to look for is rather the possession which Christian feeling and views take of previously existing customs, institutions, relationships, occupations, than the new facts and habits to which Christian feeling gives birth. It is the regenerating rather than the creative power of Christ's Spirit that He dwells upon. His Spirit, He says, does not require a new channel to be dug for it; its fuller stream may flood the old banks, may wear out corners here and there, may break out in new directions, but in the main, the channel remains the same. The man has the same arteries, but now they are filled with health-giving blood. The lump is the same lump, and done up into the same old shapes, but it is all leavened now.

The coming of the kingdom of heaven does not then consist in an entire alteration of human life, as we now know it. The kingdom of heaven comes not with observation, but is within you. It does not alter empires into republics, it does not abolish work and give us all ease, it does not find fault with the universal frame of things, or refuse to fit itself in with the world as it is; but it accepts things as it finds them, and leavens all it touches. As the outward forms of the world's business, its offices and dignities, its need of work and ways of working, would be little altered if all men were suddenly to become absolutely truthful or absolutely sober, so the change which Christ proposed to effect was of an inward, not of an outward kind. It was to be first in the individual, and only through the individual on society at large. Our Lord in establishing a kingdom on earth, did not intend to erect a vast organization over-against the world, but He meant to introduce into the world itself a leaven which should rule and subdue all to His own Spirit. The Church itself therefore may become too visible, has become in many respects too visible, and has thus unfortunately succeeded in at once separating itself from the world as a distinct and alien institution, and becoming entirely "of the world," by imitating the institutions, the ambitions, the power, the show of the world. It has learned to measure its success very largely by the bulk it occupies in the eyes of men, by its well-ordered services, its creeds and laws and courts; and it has too much forgotten that its function is of quite another kind, namely, to be *hidden* among the flour.

2. Secondly, this parable pointedly directs attention to the precise method by which the kingdom of heaven is to grow ; or, as we should more naturally say, by which the whole world is to be Christianized. To one who considers the probable future of any new or young force in the world, to one who stands beside the cradle of a new power and speculates on its future, there will occur several ways in which it may possibly prevail and attain universality. It may so commend itself to the common sense of men, or it may so appeal to their regard to their own interests, as to win universal acceptance. Railways, banks, insurance companies, do not need statutes compelling men to use them ; they win their way by their own intrinsic advantages. There have been governments so wisely administered, that men not naturally subject to them have sought to be taken under their protection for the sake of advantages accruing. Some kingdoms have thus been largely extended ; but more commonly

they have been extended by the sword, by the strong hand. Not by this latter method would Christ have His religion propagated. Yet the idea that men can somehow be compelled to accept the truth, seems never to be quite eradicated from the human mind. Very slowly is it recognized that to support a religion by any kind of force instead of by reason alone, is to admit that reason condemns it. The methods of compulsion change; the coarser forms of compulsion, the sword and the stake, give place; but more disguised and less startling forms of compulsion remain, equally opposed to the spirit of Christ.

The spread of Christianity, then, is illustrated in this parable, not by the propagation of fruit trees, nor even by the sowing of seed, but by the leavening of a mass of dough. Religion, that is to say, spreads not by a fresh sowing in each case, but by contagion. No doubt there is a direct agency of God in each case, but God works through natural means; and the natural means here pointed at is personal influence. And it is not the agency of God in the matter which our Lord wishes here to illustrate, and therefore He says nothing about it. He is not careful to guard Himself against misrepresentation by completing in every utterance a full statement of the whole truth, but presses one point at a time; and the point He here presses is, that He depends upon personal influence for the spread of His Spirit. The Church often trusts to massive and wealthy organizations, to methods which are calculated to strike every eye; but according to the Head of the Church His religion and spirit are to be propagated by an influence which operates like an infectious disease, invisible, without apparatus and pompous equipment, succeeding all the better where it is least observed. Our Lord bases His expectation of the extension of His Spirit throughout the world not upon any grand and powerful institutions, not on national establishments of religion or any such means, but on the secret, unnoticed influence of man upon man.

And indeed there exists no mightier power for good or evil than personal influence. Take even those who least intend to influence you and seem least capable of it. The little child that cannot stand alone will work that tenderness in the heart of a ruffian which no acts of parliament or prison discipline have availed to work. The wail of the suffering infant will bring a new spirit into the man whom the strongest police regulations have tended only to harden and make more defiant and embittered. By his confidence in your word, the child is a more effectual monitor of truthfulness than the keen or suspicious eye of the grown man who distrusts you: the child's recklessness of to-morrow, his short sadnesses and soon recovered smiles, his ignorance of the world and the world's misery, are the proper balance of your anxiety, and insinuate into your heart some measure of his own freshness and hope. Or what can reflect more light upon God's patience with ourselves than the unwearying love and repeated forgiveness that a child demands, and the long doubting with which we wait for the fruit of years of training? So that it is hard to say whether the parent has more influence on the child, or the child on the parent? Or take those who have been pushed aside from the busy world by ill-health or misfortune—have not their unmurmuring patience, their Christian hope, their need of our compassion, done much to mould our spirits to a sober and chastened habit? have they not imparted to us the spirit of Christ, and cherished within us a true recognition of what is essential and what accidental, what good and what evil in this world?

What, then, does the parable teach us regarding the operation of this influence? It teaches us, first, that there must be a *mixing;* that is to say, there must be contact of the closest kind between those who are and those who are not the subjects of Christ. Manifestly, no good is done by the leaven while it lies by itself; it might as well be chalk or anything else. It must be mixed with the flour. So must Christians be kneaded up together with all kinds of annoying and provoking and uncongenial people, that the spirit of Christ which they bear may become universal. Had our Lord not eaten with publicans and sinners; had He sensitively shrunk from the rough and irreverent handling He received among coarse men who called Him "Samaritan," "devil," and "sot;" had He secluded Himself in the appreciative household of Bethany; had He not made Himself the most accessible Person, little of His Spirit would have passed into other men. Other things being equal, the effect of Christian character varies with the thoroughness of the mixing. It is so with all personal influence. The depth of the love, the closeness of the intimacy, the frequency and thoroughness of the intercourse, is the measure of the effect produced. In a country such as our own, in which the population is dense, and in which an unobstructed communication subsists between man and man, things constantly tend to equalize; and what yesterday was the property of one person is to-day enjoyed by thousands. And precisely as a fashion or a contagious disease passes from man to man, with inconceivable and sometimes appalling rapidity, so does evil or good example propagate itself with as certain and speedy an increase. And this it does all the more effectually because insensibly; because we do not brace ourselves to resist this subtle atmospheric influence, nor wash our hands with any disinfectant provided against these imperceptible stains. There is no quarantine for the moral leper, nor any desert in the moral world where a man can be evil for himself alone.

For this mixing is provided for in various ways. It is provided for by *nature*, which sets us in families and mixes us up in all the familiarities and intimacies of domestic life; and by *society*, which compels us, in the prosecution of our ordinary callings, to come into contact with one another of a close and influential kind. One part of the world is "mixed" with other parts by commerce, by colonization, by conquest, so that there exists a ceaseless giving and taking of good and evil. One generation is mixed with others by reading their history and their literary remains, and by inheriting their traditions and their long established usages. So that whether we will or no this mixing goes on, and we can as little prevent certain results arising from this intercourse as we can prevent our persons from giving off heat when we enter an atmosphere colder than ourselves. We find it to be true that

> "The world's infectious: few bring back at eve
> Immaculate the manners of the morn.
> Something we thought is blotted; we resolv'd
> Is shaken; we renounced, returns again.
> Each salutation may slide in a sin
> Unthought before, or fix a former flaw."

But beyond nature's provision, beyond the *unavoidable* contact with our fellow-men to which we are all compelled, there are voluntary friendships and associations into which we enter, and casual meetings which we unawares are thrown into. Such casual and passing acquaintanceships have very frequently illustrated the truth of this parable, and have been the means of imparting the Spirit of Christ in very unlikely quarters. And it would help us to use wisely such accidental opportunities if we bore in mind that if there are to be any additions made to the kingdom of Christ, these additions are chiefly to be made from among those careless, worldly, antagonistic persons who do not at present respond to any Christian sentiments. But besides the mingling which nature, and what may be called accident, afford, there are connections we form of our own choice, and companies we enter which we might, if we chose, avoid. There is a border-land of amusements, occupations, duties, common to the godly and the ungodly, and for the regulation of our conduct, in respect to such intercourse, this parable suffices. Can the occupation be leavened, and can it be leavened by us? Can it be engaged in in a right spirit, and are we sure enough of our own stability to engage in it with benefit? A man of strong physique may scathelessly enter a room out of which a weaker constitution would inevitably carry infection. And it is foolish to argue that because some other person is none the worse of going to this or that company, or engaging in this or that pursuit, therefore you would not be the worse of it. You would not so argue if your entrance into an infected house was in question.

But there is also a culpable refusal to mix, as well as an inconsiderate eagerness to do so. Most of us shrink from the responsibility of materially influencing the life of another person. Ask a man for advice about any important matter, and you know what devices he will fall upon to avoid advising you. Many of us are really afraid of incurring the hazardous responsibility of making a man a Christian. Two opposite feelings dispose us to shrink from mingling with all kinds of people. One is a feeling of hopelessness about others. They seem so remote from the acknowledgment of Christ's rule, that we feel as if they could never be leavened. The parable reminds us, that while no doubt it is impossible to leaven sand, so long as the meal remains meal it may be leavened. The other feeling is one rather of despair about ourselves than about others. We feel as if our influence could only do harm. We are afraid to live out our inward life freely and strongly lest it injure others. This feeling, however, should prompt us neither to seclude ourselves from society, nor to behave in a constrained and artificial manner in society, but to renew our own connection with the leaven till we feel sure our whole nature is throughout renewed. If any one is exercising a healthy influence while we are languid and incapable, it is simply because that other person is in connection with Christ. That connection is open to us as well.

The mixing being thus accomplished, how is the process continued? Besides mingling with society and joining freely in all the innocent ways of the world, what is a Christian to do in order that his Christian feeling may be communicated to others? The answer is, He is to be a Christian; not to be anxious to show himself a Christian, but to be careful to be one. It has been wisely said that "the true philosophy or method of doing good is, first of all and principally, to be good—to have a character that will of itself communicate good." This is the very teaching of the parable, which says, "Be a Christian, and you must make Christians, or help to make them. Be leaven, and you will leaven." The leaven does not need to say, I am leaven; nor to say that which lies next it, Be thou leavened. By the inevitable communication of the properties of the leaven to that which lies beside it, and by this again infecting what

F

is beyond, the whole, gradually and unseen, but naturally and certainly, is leavened.

This illustration of the leaven must, of course, not be too hard pressed, as if the parable meant that only by the unconscious influence of character and not at all by the conscious and voluntary influence of speech and action, the kingdom of Christ is to be extended. Yet no one can fail to observe that the illustration of the parable is more appropriate to the unconscious than to the intended influence which Christians exercise on those around them. It is rather the all-pervading and subtle extension of Christian principles than their declared and aggressive advocacy that is brought before the mind by the figure of leaven. It reminds us that men are most susceptible to the influence that flows from character. This influence sheds itself off in a thousand ways too subtle to be resisted, and in forms so fine as to insinuate themselves where words would find no entrance. A man is in many circumstances more likely to do good by acting in a Christian manner, than by drawing attention to the faults of others and exposing their iniquity. The less ostentatious, the less conscious the influence exercised upon us is, the more likely are we to admit it. And when we are compelled to reprove, or to advise, or to entreat, this also must be in simplicity and as the natural expression, not the formal and forced exhibition of Christian feeling. The words uttered by a shallow-hearted and self-righteous Pharisee may by God's grace turn a sinner from the error of his ways; the lump of ice, itself chill and hard, may be used as a lens to kindle and thaw other objects; but notwithstanding this, he who does not speak with his whole character backing what he says, may expect to fail. It is man that influences man; not the words or individual actions of a man, but the complete character which his whole life silently reveals.

If then you sometimes reproach yourself for not exercising any perceptible influence for good over some friend or child, if it disturbs you that you have done less than you might have done by conversation or direct appeal, it may indeed be quite true that you have thus fallen short of your duty; yet remember that conduct often tells far more than talk, and that your conduct has certainly told upon the secret thoughts of your friend, whereas were you to speak merely for the sake of exonerating your conscience, the chances are, you would speak in an awkward, artificial, and ineffective manner. That conversation is often the most religious which in appearance is most secular; which concerns bills, and cargoes, and investments, and contracts, and family arrangements, and literature; and which, without any allusion to God, the soul, and eternity, secretly impregnates the whole of human life with the Spirit of Christ. If that only is to be reckoned religious conversation in which the topics of religion are discussed, then religious conversation has commonly produced more heat and bitterness and antagonism to Christ's Spirit than any other.

While, then, direct address forms one great part of the means of leavening those around you, it is to be borne in mind, that in the first place you must *be* what you wish others to become. If not, then certainly nothing that you can say is at all likely to compensate for the evil you may do by your character. It does not need that you intend evil to any; it *will be out* whether you mean it or no. If you are yourself evil, then most certainly you are making others evil. Can you number the times that you have checked the utterance of Christian feeling in those who knew they would find no response in you? Can you tell how many have been confirmed in a sinful course by your winking at their faults, and have none been led into sin by your removing the scruples of their innocence? Are you sure that your example has never turned the balance the wrong way at some critical hour of your neighbour's life? Is there no one who can stand forward and charge you with having left him in darkness about his duty, when you might have enlightened him? with having made him easy in sin by your pleasant, affable, unreproving demeanour towards him? Are there none who to all eternity will bear the punishment of sins in which you were aiding and abetting; none whom you have directly encouraged to evil, who would, but for you, have been clear of evil thoughts, desires, and deeds of which they now are guilty; none in whose punishment you might see the punishment of sins which were as much yours as theirs, and the memory of which might seem sufficient, if that were possible, to poison the very joys of heaven?

Do not turn the warning of this parable aside by the thought, 'Am I my brother's keeper? Most assuredly you are responsible for your own character, and for all its effects. If you are not doing good to others, it is because there is something wrong in yourself. If you are not leavening others, it is because you are yourself unleavened: for there is no such thing as leaven that does not impart its qualities to that which is about it. Can you confine the perfume to the flower, or restrict the light of the sun to its own globe? Just as little can you restrain all Christian qualities within your own person: something material, something essential to Christian character is lacking if it be not influencing those about it.

It is a glorious consummation that this parable speaks of. It tells of a mixing that is to go on till "*the whole*" is leavened. The Spirit of Christ is to pervade all things. That Spirit is to take possession of all national characteristics and all individual gifts. Every variety of quality, of human faculty, temperament, and endowment, is to be Christianized, that all may serve Christ. In His kingdom is to be gathered all that has ever served or gladdened humanity: the freshness of childhood and its simplicity, the sagacity, gravity, and self-command of age, the enterprise and capacity of manhood, the qualities that suffering matures, and those that are nurtured by prosperity; all occupations that have invited and stimulated and rewarded the energies of men, all modes of human life, and all affections that conscience approves, all that is the true work, joy, and glory, of our nature is to be pervaded with the sanctifying, purifying, elevating leaven of Christ's Spirit. And this is to be achieved not otherwise than by personal influence. Is it possible that you should have no desire to help in this? that you should be in the world of men and not care to see it accomplishing this destiny? that you should know the earnestness of Christ in this behalf, and never lift a finger or open your lips to aid Him? Surely it will pain you to come to the end of life and have it to reflect that not one soul has been effectually helped by you. Would you not save many if by a wish you could lift them to the gate of heaven? Is it, then, because of the little labour and sacrifice that are needed for this purpose that you hold back from helping? Is there nothing you can do, is there nothing you ought to do in the way of leavening some little bit of the great mass? Come back yourselves to the leaven, cultivate diligently that fellowship with Christ Himself, which is alone sufficient to equip you for this great calling. Make sure of the reality of your own acceptance of His Spirit, and then whatever you do, utter, touch, will all be leavéned.

V.

THE HID TREASURE AND THE PEARL OF PRICE.

"*Again, the kingdom of heaven is like unto treasure hid in a field; the which when a man hath found, he hideth, and for joy thereof goeth and selleth all that he hath, and buyeth that field. Again, the kingdom of heaven is like unto a merchant man, seeking goodly pearls: who, when he had found one pearl of great price, went and sold all that he had, and bought it.*"—MATT. xiii. 44-46.

THE HID TREASURE AND THE PEARL OF PRICE.

MATT. xiii. 44-46.

THESE two parables have one and the same object. They are meant to exhibit the incomparable value of the kingdom of heaven. They exhibit this value not by attempting to describe the kingdom or its various advantages, but by depicting the eagerness with which he who finds it and recognises its value, parts with all to make it his own. This eagerness is not dependent on the previous expectations or views or condition of the finder of the kingdom, but is alike displayed whether the finder is lifted by his discovery out of acknowledged poverty, or has his hands already filled with goodly pearls; whether he has no outlook and hope at all, or is eagerly seeking for perfect happiness. The one parable illustrates the eagerness of a poor man who lights upon the treasure apparently by accident; the other illustrates the eagerness of a rich man whose finding of the pearl of price is the result of carefully studied and long sustained search.

This difference in the two parables sets clearly before the mind a distinction which is frequently apparent among those who become Christians. Men naturally view life very differently, and take up from the first very various attitudes towards the world into which we all have come. One person is from the first quite at home in it, another slinks through it as if there were nothing friendly or congenial to him here. One man seems to regard it as a banquetting house which is to be made the most of ere the sun rise and dispel his illusion, while another uses it as a battlefield where conquests are to be made, and where all is to be done in grim earnest and strenuously with no thought of pleasure. And, as these parables indicate, there are men born with placid and contented natures, others with eager, soaring, insatiable spirits; some, in a word, are born merchants, others day-labourers. Some, that is, are born with a noble instinct which never forsakes them, but prompts them to believe that there is infinite joy and satisfaction to be found, and that it shall be theirs: they cannot rest with small things, but are driven always forwards to more and higher. Others, again, never look beyond their present attainment, cannot understand the restless ambition that weeps for more worlds, have no speculation in them, no broad plan of life, nor much idea that any purpose is to be served by it. They have the peaceful, happy industry which makes the day's labour easy, but not the enterprize which can plan a life's work and make every available material on earth subserve its plan.

This difference, when exhibited in connection with religion, becomes very marked. Looking upon some men, you would say you don't know how ever they are to be brought to Christ, they are so thoroughly at home and at rest in their daily business, and this seems to afford them so much interest, satisfaction, and reward that you cannot fancy them so much as once reflecting whether something more is not needed. They seem so peculiarly fitted for this world, you can fancy them going on in the same sphere for ever. Of others, again, you are perpetually wondering how they have not long ago found what they have been so long seeking; you know that, employ themselves as they will in this world, their inward thought is writing vanity on all this world gives them — they crave a spiritual treasure.

In the first of these two parables, then, we see how the kingdom of heaven is sometimes found by those who are not seeking it. The point of this part of the parable and its distinction from the other seems to lie in this, that while the man was giving a deeper furrow to his field, intent only on his team, his ploughshare suddenly grated on the slab that concealed or rung upon the chest that contained the treasure, or turned up a glittering coin that had fallen out in the hasty burial of the store. Or he may have been sauntering through a neighbour's field, when his eye is suddenly attracted by some sign which makes his heart leap to his mouth and fixes him for the moment to the spot, because he knows that treasure must be there. He went out in the morning thinking of nothing less than that before nightfall his fortune would be made—suddenly, without effort or expectation of his, he sees untold wealth within his grasp. He knows nothing of the history of the treasure—does not know on whose feet these bright anklets gleamed in the dance, knows none of the touching memories that are associated with that signet ring, nothing of the long hard strife by which these gold-pieces were acquired, nor of the disaster which tore them from the reluctant hand of the possessor. It is not *his* blood that has dyed the gold on that jewel-hilted scimitar. He can imagine the careworn man when trouble and war overran the land, stealing out in the darkness and making his treasure secure, and marking it by signs which, alas! he was never again to note; but he *knows* nothing of him, knew nothing of him. Ages before, this treasure had been hid; for him it had been prepared without any intention or labour of his, and now suddenly he lights upon it; out of poverty he to his own astonishment steps into wealth, and his whole life is changed for him without hope or effort of his own.

So, says our Lord, is the kingdom of heaven. Suddenly, in the midst of other thoughts a man is brought face to face with Christ, and while earning his daily bread and seeking for no more than success in life can give him, unexpectedly finds that eternal things are his. Christ is found of them that sought Him not. Is it not often so? The man has begun life not thinking that any very great thing can be made of it, as little as the ploughman expects to be lord of the manor, and to own the horses, lands, and comforts of the proprietor. He begins with the idea that if he is careful, diligent, and favoured by circumstances, life may be pleasant. He has a prospect of a decent, comfortable livelihood, or, at the best, of a good-going business, with margin of leisure for friendly intercourse, the reading of pleasant literature, and so on. He is confident he will marry happily, and live and see good days. In other words, he has extremely modest expectations of what life can do for him; has no soaring anticipations of "the ampler aether, the diviner air," does not recognise his own capacity nor the size he may grow to, but, like the child for whom the world can do no more if he is promised some favourite toy, fancies that no better thing can come to him than houses, lands, wife and children, friendships and prosperity. Or if he once had visitings of a higher, ampler hope, and seemed to see that round and beyond the successes of business and the common pleasures of life there lay a limitless ocean of feeling and of thought,—worlds upon worlds, like the starry unfathomable firmament, in which the soul might find expanse and joy for ever,—these visions have been wiped out by the coarse hand of some early sin, or have been worn from the surface of the mind by the hard traffic of the world; and now what the shrivelled creature seeks is possibly but the accomplishment of a daily routine, possibly the attainment of some poor ambition, or the wreaking of a low revenge, or triumph over a rival who has defeated him, or possibly not even anything so definite as that. He *had* a vision of a life which might fulfil high aims, which might be ennobled and glorified throughout by true and pervading fellowship with God, he once was confident that what the human imagination could conceive of good, that, and far more than that, was possible to the human nature, and to every man who had it; but that bright vision has passed as the morning, all aglow with light and freshness, is quenched in rain and cloud and gloomy wretchedness.

This, then, is in point of fact the condition of many a man as he passes through life—he has no conception of the blessedness that awaits him, he has as little hope of any supreme and complete felicity as the man of the parable had any expectation of lighting upon a hid treasure. We only think of what *we* can make of life, not of the wealth God has laid in our path. But suddenly our steps are arrested ; circumstances that seem purely accidental break down the partition that has hemmed us in to time, and we see that eternity is ours. We thought we had a house, 100 acres of land, £1000 well invested, and we find we have God. We were comforting ourselves with the prospect of increased salary, of ampler comforts and advantages, and a voice comes ringing through our soul, " *all things* are yours, for ye are Christ's and Christ is God's." *How* it is that the eyes are now opened to this treasure, we can as little tell as the ploughman who has driven his slow steers over that same field since first he could guide the plough but has never till this day seen the treasure. A few words casually dropped, a sentence read in an idle moment, some break in our prosperous course, some pause which allows the mind to wander in unaccustomed directions,— one cannot say what is insufficient to bring the wandering and empty soul to a settled possession of the kingdom of heaven, for the treasure seems to be his before he looks for it, before he feels his need of it, before he has taken thought or steps about it. This morning he was content with what a man can have outside of God's kingdom: this evening everything outside that kingdom has lost its value and is as nothing. The man who is lost in mist on a wild hill thinks himself exceptionally well off if he can find a sheepfold to give him shelter, and is thankful if he can see two steps before him and can avoid the precipice; but suddenly the sun shines out, the mist lifts, and he sees before him a boundless prospect, bright placid dwellings of men, and his path leading down to the shining valley with all its stir of life, and now what comforted and sufficed him before is all forgotten.

You will not fail in passing to draw the inference from this presentation of the manner of finding the kingdom, that conversions which have taken place quite unexpectedly and with great ease on the part of the converted person, need not therefore be insufficient and hollow. We are very apt to think that because the kingdom of heaven is so great a treasure a man should spend much labour in attaining it—that as the acceptance of Christ is the most important attainment a man can make, there ought to be some proportionate effort and expectancy on his part—that so great a treasure is not to be made over to one who is not caring for it or thinking of it. But this parable shows us that there may be a finding without any previous seeking, and that the essential thing is, not whether a man has been seeking, and how long, and how earnestly—no, but whether a man has found. The man in the parable would not have found more in that spot had he been seeking more and seeking it elsewhere all his days; the buried money was not accumulating interest while he was spending years in the search. The very same treasure may be found by the man who has grown gray in the quest of treasure, and by the child who plays in the field; by the alchemist who has spent his life in examining the boasted tests for finding treasure, and by the labouring man who has never heard of such tests and does not dream of finding sudden wealth. The question is, Does a man know the value of what has turned up before him, and is he so in earnest as to sell all for it? Let us not hesitate to believe that in one hour some heedless person has found what we have all our life been seeking, if only he shows his appreciation of the treasure by parting with all for it.

The second parable introduces us to the other, the higher type of man, the merchantman—the man who has *not* moderate expectations, who refuses ever to be satisfied until he has all, who is always meditating new ventures, and to whom his present possessions are only of value as the means of acquiring what is yet beyond his reach. He sets out with the inborn conviction or instinct that there *is* something worth seeking, worth the labour and the search of a life, something which will abundantly repay us, and to which we can wholly, freely, and eternally give ourselves up, and on which we shall delight to spend our whole strength, capabilities, and life. He refuses to be satisfied with the moderate, often interrupted and often quenched joys of this life. He considers physical health, the respect of his fellow-men, a good education, good social position, and so forth, as all goodly pearls, but he is not going to sit down satisfied with these things if there is anything better to be had. He refuses to have anything short of the best. He goes on from one acquirement to another. Money is good, he at first thinks, but knowledge is better. He parts with the one to get the other. Friendship is good, but love is better, and he cannot satisfy himself with the one, but must also have the other. The respect of his fellows is good, but self-respect and a pure conscience are better. Human love is a goodly pearl, but this only quickens him to crave insatiably for the love of God. He must always have what is beyond and best. He refuses to believe that God has created us to be partially satisfied, happy at intervals, content with effort, *believing* ourselves blessed, disguising the reality of our condition by the aid of fancy, or fleeing from it on the wings of hope, but to be partakers of His own blessedness, and to enjoy eternally the sufficiency of Him in whom are all things.

This spirit of expectation is encouraged by the parable. It seems to say to us, Covet earnestly the best gifts. Never make up your mind merely to endure or merely to be resigned. Test what you have, and if it do not satisfy you wholly, seek for something better. It is not for you who have a God, a God of infinite resource and of infinite love, to accustom yourselves to merely negative blessings and doubtful, limited conditions. You are to start with the belief that you are not made for final disappointment, nor to rest content with something less than you once hoped for or can now conceive, but that there is somewhere, and attainable by you, the most unchallengeable felicity—that there does exist a perfect condition, a pearl of great price, and that there is but a question of the way to it, a question of search. You are to start with this belief, and you are to hold to it to the end. Under no compulsion or enticement, in the face of no disappointment, give up this persuasion that goodly pearls are to be had, and to be had by you, that into your life and soul the full sense of ample possession is one day to enter. When you come up from a breathless eager search like the pearl-diver, spent and bleeding, and with your hands filled only with mud or worthless shells; or when, like the merchant, you have ventured your all, and are reduced to beggary and thrown back to the very beginning, the great hope of your life being taken from you; when all your days seem to have been wasted in fruitless search; when every feeling within you rises up in mutiny against you, and like an ignorant crew scorns your adventure, and would put about and run with the wind back from the new world you seek, put them down; you have certainty on your side, simple, sheer certainty, for "he that seeketh, *findeth.*"

The important point in these parables is that which is common to both. The teaching which our Lord desires to convey by their means regards the incomparable value of the kingdom of heaven, and the readiness with which one who perceives its value will give up all for it. He wishes us to consider the alacrity, gladness, and assurance with which one who apprehends the value of the kingdom will and should put aside everything which prevents him from making it his own. It is the usual, universal, mercantile feeling. The merchant does not part with his other possessions reluctantly when he wishes to obtain some better possession; he longs to get rid of them; he goes into the investment about which he has satisfied himself with thorough good will; he clears out as fast as he can from every other investment, and endeavours to realize wherever he can that he may have his means free for this better and more productive venture. People who do not know its value may think the man mad selling out at low prices, at unsuitable times, at a loss; but he knows what he is doing. I don't care what I lose, he says to himself, for if I can only get that field I shall have infinite compensation for my losses. As soon as he has made up his mind that there *is* a treasure in the field, he is filled with tremulous, sleepless eagerness, till he makes it his own. Day and night his heart is there and his thoughts. His dreams are full of visions of possession, or of heart-breaking failure. His waking hours are nervously agitated by fears and schemings. He always finds that his road home lies past the longed-for property. He is jealous of the very birds that hover over it. The world is full of stories, and every day adds to the stock of stories that display the ingenuity, craft, perseverance, consuming zeal, spent in winning the bit of ground that is coveted. No labour is grudged, no sacrifice is shrunk from, no present poverty is a trial if it brings the coveted property nearer.

But is this a similitude for the kingdom of heaven? Is it not rather a picture of what ought to be than of what is? What we commonly find is that the kingdom of heaven is not so esteemed. We see men hesitating to part with anything for it, looking at it as a sad alternative, as a resort to which they must perhaps betake themselves when too old to enjoy life any longer, as what they may have to come to when all the real joy and intensity of life are gone, but not as that on which life itself can best be spent. Entrance into the kingdom of heaven is looked upon much as entrance into the fortified town is viewed by the rural population. It may be necessary in time of danger, but they will think with longing of the fields and homesteads they must abandon; it is by constraint, not from love, that they make the change. In short, it is plain that men generally do not reckon the kingdom of heaven to be of such value that they sacrifice everything else for its sake. And it is of supreme importance that we should clearly see the grounds on which we base our confidence that we ourselves are exceptions to the general rule, if we have such a confidence. Have we really shown any of that mercantile eagerness which the parable speaks of? Have we in any way shown that the kingdom of heaven is first in our thoughts? What meaning has this "selling of all" in our life?

For it is to be observed that there always is this selling wherever the kingdom is won. We have it not at all unless we have given all for it. It is like a choice between living in the town or in the country. We know we cannot do both, and in order to secure the advantages of the one kind of life we must give up those of the other. So, living for ourselves prevents us from living for God, and we cannot do the one without wholly giving up the other. If you value the kingdom of God more than all else, you will eagerly give up everything that prevents your winning it; but no mere pretended esteem for it will prompt you to make the needful sacrifices, or will actually give you possession. If you do not really desire the kingdom more than aught else, then you have not found it. A feigned desire does not move us to obtain anything. It is what you really love that you spend thought and effort and money upon, not what you know you ought to love, and are trying to persuade yourself to love.

In conclusion, this parable lets fall these two words of warning—1. Make your calculations, and act accordingly. If you think the world will pay you better than Christ, then serve it; give yourself heartily and without compunction to it. Do not be so weak as to allow thoughts of things eternal and a spiritual world you have forsaken to haunt you and spoil your enjoyment.

Make your choice and act upon it. If there is no better pearl, no richer treasure than what you can win by devotion to business and living for yourself, then by all means choose that, and make the most of it. But if you think that Christ was right, if you foresee that what is outside His kingdom must perish, and that He has gathered within it all that is worthy, all that is enduring, all that is as it ought to be, if you know that you are not and can never be blessed outside that kingdom, then let the reasonableness and remonstrance of this parable move you to show some eagerness in winning that great treasure. Make your choice and act upon it. Let your mind dwell on the objects Christ has in view till you become enamoured of them, and till they alone draw you and command your effort. Strive to shake off the pitiful avarice, the timorous anxieties, the cowardly self-seeking, the low, earthly, stupid aims of the man who serves the world, and let the Spirit of Christ draw you into fellowship with His aims, and give you a place in His kingdom.

2. If you have this treasure, do not murmur at the price you have paid for it. If you have to forego earthly advancement, if you are inwardly constrained to part with money which might have brought many comforts, if you have been drawn to do things which are misconstrued and which make you feel awkward with your

friends, if self asserts itself again and again, and claims pleasure and gain and gratification of various kinds, do not murmur at what the kingdom is costing you, but rather count over your treasure, and see how much more you have than you have lost. Having what worlds cannot buy, you will surely not vex yourself by longing for this or that which the poorest-spirited slave of this world can easily obtain. Suppose you had the offer to barter your interest in the kingdom for any or all of the possessions, advantages, and pleasures you are deprived of, you would not do it; if, then, in your own judgment and by your own deliberate choice you have the better portion, it is scarcely fair to bewail yourself as an ill-used person. Anything you have been required to give up for the kingdom's sake was either of no real value—it was the coin which, so long as you kept it, could neither warm nor clothe you, and whose only use was to buy valuables; or if of real value, the relinquishment of it has given you what is of infinite value.

VI.

THE NET.

"Again, the kingdom of heaven is like unto a net, that was cast into the sea, and gathered of every kind: which, when it was full, they drew to shore, and sat down, and gathered the good into vessels, but cast the bad away. So shall it be at the end of the world: the angels shall come forth, and sever the wicked from among the just, and shall cast them into the furnace of fire: there shall be wailing and gnashing of teeth."—MATT. xiii. 47-50.

THE NET.

MATT. xiii. 47-50.

IN the foregoing parables of the kingdom Jesus has pointed out the causes of its success and failure, its mixed appearance in this world, its surprising growth from small beginnings, and the method of its extension. He now points to the result of all, when the great net shall be drawn to shore, all the influences and efforts of this life ended and brought to a pause; when there shall be "no more sea," no fluctuation, no ebb and flow, no tide of good resolve and progress sucked back from all it had reached, and leaving a foul and slimy beach; especially no mingling of bad and good in an obscure and confusing element; but decision and separation, a deliberate sitting down to see what has been made of this world by us all, and a summing up on that eternal shore of all gains and results, and every man's aim made manifest by his end.

There is obviously considerable resemblance between this parable of the net and the parable of the tares. But the one is not a mere repetition of the other under a different figure.

Every parable is intended to illustrate one truth. Light may incidentally be shed on other points, as you cannot turn your eye or the light you carry on the object you wish to examine without seeing and shedding light on other things as well. Now the one truth which is especially enforced in the parable of the tares is that it is dangerous in the extreme to attempt in this present time to separate the evil from the good in the Church: whereas the one truth to which the parable of the net gives prominence is that this separation will be effected by and by in its own suitable time. No doubt this future separation appears in the parable of the tares also, but in that parable it is introduced for the sake of lending emphasis to the warning against attempting a separation now: in this parable of the net it is introduced with no such purpose. A weeding process might very naturally suggest itself, indeed always does suggest itself, to one looking over a hedge at a dirty field; but no one watching the drawing of a net would dream of plunging in to throw out worthless fish. Let the net be drawn; then, as a matter of course, the separation will be made. The value of the take, which cannot yet be estimated, will be ascertained by and by. The whole results of the work of Christ in the world will then but not sooner be known.

Another point of distinction between the two

parables is this, that while in the one parable the springing of tares among the good corn is ascribed to the design of an enemy, in the other the mixture of good and bad in the net is rather exhibited as necessarily resulting from the nature of the case. In hunting, a man can make his choice and pick out the finest of the herd, letting the rest go; but in fishing with a net no such selection is possible; all must be drawn to shore that happens to have been embraced within the sweep of the net. So in sending out His servants to invite men to the kingdom, our Lord did not name individuals to whom they were to go, and who should, from first to last, prove themselves obedient to the word; He did not even name classes of persons or races with whom they would be sure to find success, but He told them to go into all the world and invite all men without distinction. The preachers of the kingdom have no powers to make selections for God; and to say of one that he will be, and of another that he will never be valuable to God. They are to cast the net so as to embrace all, and leave the determination of what is bad and what is good to the end.

Before endeavouring to extract from the parable its direct teaching, one cannot fail to notice some more general ideas suggested by the figure used. We are, for example, reminded that we are all advancing through life towards its final issue. Our condition in this respect bears a close resemblance to fish enclosed in a net. You have seen men dragging a river, fixing one end of the net, taking the other across the whole stream, and then fetching a wide compass, and enclosing in their net everything dead or alive, bad or good, from surface to bottom. Or you have seen the same thing done in the sea, one net enclosing quite a lake within itself, and gradually as it closes round the fish, and they find that it is sunk to the sand and floated to the crest of the wave, you have pitied their wild efforts to escape, and seen how sure a barrier these imperceptible meshes are. At first, while the net is wide, they frisk and leap and seem free, but soon they discover that their advance is but in one direction, and when they halt they feel the pressure of the net. So is it with ourselves—we *must* go on, we cannot break through into the past, we cannot ever again be at the same distance from the shore as we were last year, yesterday, now. Yesterday, however delightful, you cannot live twice; eternity, however distasteful, you are certainly going on to. This day you have less space and scope than ever you had before, and every hour you spend, every action you do, every pleasure you enjoy makes this little space less. You cannot make time stand still till you shall resolve how to spend it. You cannot bring your life to a pause while you make experiments as to the best mode of living. The years you spend ill, you cannot receive again to spend well; the years spent in indecision, in doubt, in selfish seclusion *are* spent, and cannot now be filled with service of God and profit to your fellows. Your lifetime you have but once, and each hour of it but once; and as remorselessly as the last night of the convicted criminal is beat out and brings round the morning that is to look upon his death, so are your lives running steadily out, never faster when you long for to morrow, never slower when you fear it, but ever with the same measured and certain advance. Do what you will, make what plans you will, settle yourself as fixedly in this life as you will, you are passing through and out of it, and shall one day look on it as all past—for ever past. By no will of our own have we come into this life, but here we find ourselves and the net fallen behind us, so that we must accept all the responsibilities of human life, and go on to meet all its consequences.

Besides enclosure and inevitable passing on to a termination, the net suggests the idea of entanglement. Looking at fish in a net you see many that are not swimming freely, but are caught in the meshes and dragged on. The experience of some persons interprets this to them. While all of us are drawing on together towards eternity there are some who feel daily the pressure of the net. They have got into circumstances which they would fain be out of but cannot. Their position is not altogether of their own choosing, and they discharge its duties because they must, not because they would. At some former period they were too careless, or shortsighted, or irresolute; they exercised too little their right to determine their own course, and they now suffer the bondage consequent on this neglect.

If the conduct required of you by the position or connection into which you have come be disapproved by your conscience, then you must somehow break through and escape, else your soul will suffer detriment, and that in you which was good when first you were entangled will be landed broken, bruised, and useless. But if the conduct required be only disagreeable and humiliating and not sinful, you may have to adjust yourself to your circumstances. Do not toss and struggle in the net, but quietly set yourself to make the most of the condition you have unfortunately brought yourself into. It may now be your duty to continue in a position it was not your duty originally to enter. A wrong choice may have brought you to a right thing. Do not, therefore, allow any feeling of the awkwardness, restrictions, unsuitableness, or painfulness of your position, nor any reflections on the folly that brought you into it, to fret you into uselessness. Just because it seems in so many ways unsuitable, it may call out deeper qualities in you, a patience which otherwise might have been undeveloped, a knowledge of God and man, a meekness and strength, which enlarge and mature your spirit.

Under very strange influences and forces are we passing onwards; by hopes and ambitions, by sickness and watching, by anguish and mirth, by the forlorn remembrance of a happy past and the sad forecasting of the future, by occupations that hurry us on from day to day, and by longings that abide with us through life and are never satisfied. And often we would fain escape from the gentle compulsion by which God draws us to our end, and have to remind ourselves that however entangled and tied up we are, and however prevented from our own ways and directions, this present time is after all but the drawing of the net and not the time of our use; that though now debarred from many pursuits we think we might be useful in, and hurried past enjoyments that delight us, we are passing to a shore where there is room and time enough for the fulfilment of every human purpose and the exercise of every human faculty; that after all our sins and follies, after all our pains and anxieties and difficulties, there does most surely come the kingdom of heaven and its glorious liberty. Here we quickly wax old, our freedom of choice and liberty of action are quickly taken from us, we stretch forth our hands and another girds us and carries us whither we would not; but there our youth shall be renewed with all its freedom from care, its spring and energy, its fresh views of truth, its boldness to live and see good days, its purpose for the life that lies before it unsullied; and it shall be again as when "thou wast young and girdedst thyself and walkedst whither thou wouldest."

But these are not the points emphasised in the parable. The parable sets the present mixture of good and bad in the kingdom of heaven or in the Church over against the eventual separation.

1. First then, we have the truth that the net gathers "of every kind." This is the first thing that strikes one looking at a net drawn ashore—the confused mass of dead and living rubbish and prize. Shells, mud, starfish, salt-smelling weed, useless refuse of all kinds, are mingled with the fresh and wholesome fish that lie gasping and floundering in the net. Of the bad there is every kind of thing that can spoil the net and injure its contents; and of the good there is every kind, small and great, coarse and fine. And until the net is fairly landed it is impossible to say whether the weight is to be rejoiced in or

not. This is set before us as a picture of the Church of Christ as it now is. It embraces every variety of character. At one time we are tempted to think that the mass of professing Christians is but so much dead weight; at other times we measure the success of the gospel by the mere numbers brought within the Church. The truth is, we cannot yet say much about the success of the gospel. Occasionally indeed there may be a gleam through the water that gives assurance of a large and fine fish: there may be deeds done which draw the eye of every one, and unmistakably prove that in the Church there are men after God's own heart. We feel that of some men the character and quality are already ascertained, and that it needs no day of separation to tell us their worth. But there remains a vast mass about which we can say little; nay, we know that in the Church there are foul, lumpish, poisonous creatures. This is what our Lord anticipated, that while His Church would attract men whom God would gather to Him with delight as being of His own spirit, there would also be drawn to it a number of wretched creatures who would go through life trying to hide from themselves that they love the world much more than God, and who must in the end be thrown aside as fit for no good purpose, as so much useless rubbish.

This mixture arises from the manner in which

the kingdom of heaven is proclaimed among men. It is not proclaimed by addressing private messages to selected and approved individuals, but publicly to all. And it is so proclaimed because it is for men generally and not for any special kind or class, and because God "would have all men to be saved." The recruiting sergeant watches for likely men and singles them out from the crowd; but the kingdom of heaven opens its gates to all, because it has that which appeals to humanity at large, and can make use of every kind of man who honestly attaches himself to it. Our freedom of choice is left absolutely uncontrolled so far as the outward offer of the gospel goes; it is not even biassed by any knowledge on our part that we are considered specially suitable for the work God has to do. Christ's kingdom gathers in not only those in whom there is a natural leaning towards a devout life, or those who are of a susceptible temperament, or those who are attracted by a life of self-sacrifice, but it gathers in "of every kind." You really cannot say who among your friends is most likely to become a Christian, because men become Christians not from any apparent predisposition, not because religion suits their idiosyncrasy, their individual mood and special tastes, but because the kingdom of heaven satisfies human wants which are as common to the race as hunger and thirst. But the kingdom being thus open to all, many enter it for the sake of some of its advantages, while they remain at heart disloyal, and are never carried out of themselves by a sense of its glory, and are alien to that great movement for the lasting good of men which the kingdom truly is. They have an external present attachment to the kingdom, but they do not belong to it and are not in it heart and soul.

But this mixture is at length to give place. In the net, while we are in this world, all distinctions seem to be made light of; in the end, on the shore, a final and real distinction is to be exhibited and acted on. All are to pass through the hands of skilled judgment. The angels sever the wicked from among the just, so that the just alone are left in the net. The purpose of the net, of the draught, of the whole ongoing of this world is at length seen to have been for the sake of the just. Much bulkier, weightier, noisier, brighter-coloured, more curious things are drawn up, but these are cast aside summarily —it was not to secure these the net was drawn. The fishermen were not mere naturalists dragging for what is curious and rare; not mere idlers fishing for sport and caring little for the *use* of the result; not mere children amazed and delighted with every strange or huge thing they land ; but they have cast the net for a purpose, and whatever is not suitable for this purpose is refuse and rubbish to them. The huge creature that has been a terror to the deep, the lovely sea plant that has waved its fruitless head in the garden of the sea—these are not twice looked at by the fishermen. They are acting on an understanding that the net was drawn for a purpose.

And so it shall be in the end of the world. The *end* is not a mere running down of the machinery that keeps the world going, it is not a mere exhaustion of the life that keeps us all alive, it is not a hap-hazard cutting of the thread; it is a conclusion, coming as truly in its own fit day and order, as much in the fulness of time and because things are ripe for it, as the birth of Christ came. It is the time of the gathering up of all things to completion, when the few last finishing strokes are given to the work, that suddenly show the connection of things which seemed widely separate, and reveal at once the purpose and meaning of the whole. Men will then understand, what now scarcely one can constantly believe, that it is God's purpose that is silently being accomplished, and that it is usefulness to Him that is the final standard of value.

The distinction which finally separates men into two classes must be real and profound. It is here said to be *our value to God*. Are we useless to Him, or can He make us serve any good purpose? Have we become so wholly demoralized by a selfish, limited life, that we cannot cherish any cordial desire for the common good, or enter into sympathy with purposes that do not promise profit or pleasure to ourselves? You have some idea what the purposes of God are; you see these purposes in the life and death of Christ; you know that in God's purposes that which contributes to the elevation of character takes precedence of what merely secures outward comfort or present advantage; you recognise that His Spirit delights in deeds of mercy, of self-sacrifice, of holy service—have you, then, such qualities as would be helpful in carrying out such purposes? are you already influential in society for good, helpful in extirpating vice and crime, and in alleviating the wretchedness of disease and poverty? do your sympathies and your thoughts run much towards such an expenditure of your energies? have you the first requisite of His servants, such a participation in His love for men, and such a zeal for the advancement of the race as wither within you all isolating and debasing selfishness?

The fish taken in the net are disposed of by the fishermen, and are in their hands without choice or motion. A minute before, they were swimming hither and thither, moving themselves by their own energies; now they are dealt with according to a judgment not their own. The situation is not more novel to the fishes than it will be to us. Here in this world, we are conscious of a power to choose our own destiny, to change our character, and become different from what we are. We are not yet all we ought to be, but we can discard evil habits, repress base motives, and become at length suitable for God's work, harmonious with Him through all our being. So we flatter ourselves. But there comes a time, when, whatever we are, that we shall for ever be; when we shall be, as it were, passive in the grip of destiny, disposed of by it, and unable to resist or alter it; when we shall find that the time for choosing is past, and that we must accept and abide by the consequences of our past choices; when for us the irrevocable word shall have gone forth, "He that is filthy, let him be filthy still; and he that is holy, let him be holy still."

Amidst the sudden revolutions of thought and revulsions of feeling, amidst the utter discomfiture of many a hope on that day when the net is drawn and we are all suddenly thrown out on the eternal shore, will your hope not fail you? As you anticipate the hand that is to separate the good from the bad, do you rejoice that a penetrating eye and an unerring wisdom will guide it? do you rejoice that it is God who is coming to judge the world in righteousness, and that no mistake can be made, no superficial distinction hide the real one?

It is possible some one may defend himself against the parable by saying, "I will not alarm myself by judging of my destiny by my own qualities; I am trusting to Christ." But precisely in so far as you are trusting to Christ, you have those qualities which the final judgment will require you to show. "If any man hath not the Spirit of Christ, he is none of His." You are useful to God in so far as you have the Spirit of Christ. Plainly the criterion given by the parable is the only sufficient criterion by which men can be judged as they issue from this life. Are they in such sympathy with God as to be capable of entering into His work and ways in the future, or have they only cultivated habits and qualities which served them for a life that is now past? Only by what we are, can we be finally judged; not by what we believe, but by what our belief has made us; not by what we profess, not by what we know, but by the results in character of what we have professed and known. In the final judgment, we shall not be required to assert that we are converted persons, or that we are trusting in Christ; we shall not be required to assert any thing; but our future shall be determined by our actual fitness for it. Fitness for carrying on God's work in the future, fitness for helping forward the cause of humanity in the future, fitness for living in and finding our joy in the future which Christ's Spirit is to rule, we must have if we are to enter that future. Get the fitness how you may, it is this you must have. If you can get it by some other means than by adherence to Christ and the reception of His Spirit, use that means, but this fitness you must have.

And I think any one who seriously accepts this as the real outlook for us men will feel that he cannot do better than go to school to Christ, that he may acquire not only a perception of what this fitness is, but that genuine humility and absorption in great and eternal aims which are its prime requisites. Apart from Christ, men may be good handicraftsmen, they may be gifted with genius that delights and aids mankind and beautifies life, they may see clearly what constitutes civil prosperity, in one way or other they may materially help forward the common cause; but if after all they are not in sympathy with the purpose of the King who rules and heads the forward movement, if their motives in using their gifts are still selfish, it can never be said to them, "Enter thou into the joy of thy Lord." His joy is a joy they are not prepared to share, if they have sought their own advantage and not with Him sacrificed themselves to the common good. It is impossible to say who are helping and who are hindering the cause of Christ; and happily it is not our part to judge. The aims and ideas which Christ introduced to the minds of men have so permeated society that no one can grow up in a Christian country without coming more or less in contact with them. And the Spirit of Christ may have wrought in men in ways we are quite unable to trace. But it would seem as if only through Christ it were possible for us to come into that full sympathy at once with God and with men, which we see so clearly in His life and death, and which also is our salvation from selfish isolation and all ungodliness and inhumanity. It is serviceableness which is to determine our entrance into or exclusion from the future of God; or, as God does not desire service in which is no spirit of fellowship, but rather the intelligent and delighted co-operation of sons, it is sonship that determines our destiny. And who but Christ enables us to see what sonship is and to become sons? How is that tender, humble, sin-fearing, reverent spirit of God's children to be produced, how has it ever been produced, save by the acceptance of Christ as God the Son dying for our sin to bring us to the Father?

VII.

THE UNMERCIFUL SERVANT OR THE UNFORGIVING DEBTOR.

"Therefore is the kingdom of heaven likened unto a certain king, which would take account of his servants. And when he had begun to reckon, one was brought unto him, which owed him ten thousand talents. But forasmuch as he had not to pay, his lord commanded him to be sold, and his wife, and children, and all that he had, and payment to be made. The servant therefore fell down, and worshipped him, saying, Lord, have patience with me, and I will pay thee all. Then the lord of that servant was moved with compassion, and loosed him, and forgave him the debt. But the same servant went out, and found one of his fellowservants, which owed him an hundred pence: and he laid hands on him, and took him by the throat, saying, Pay me that thou owest. And his fellowservant fell down at his feet, and besought him, saying, Have patience with me, and I will pay thee all. And he would not: but went and cast him into prison, till he should pay the debt. So when his fellowservants saw what was done, they were very sorry, and came and told unto their lord all that was done. Then his lord, after that he had called him, said unto him, O thou wicked servant, I forgave thee all that debt, because thou desiredst me: shouldest not thou also have had compassion on thy fellowservant, even as I had pity on thee? And his lord was wroth, and delivered him to the tormentors, till he should pay all that was due unto him. So likewise shall my heavenly Father do also unto you, if ye from your hearts forgive not every one his brother their trespasses."—MATT. xviii. 23-35.

THE UNMERCIFUL SERVANT;
OR,
THE UNFORGIVING DEBTOR.

MATT. xviii. 23-35.

THE occasion of this parable was a question put by Peter. Our Lord has once again been warning His disciples against that self-sufficient spirit which makes men quarrelsome and implacable and censorious. Their ambitious temper had been again showing itself in the discussion of their favourite topic: "Who is the greatest in the kingdom of heaven?" They had been betraying their eagerness to be influential and important persons, their proneness therefore to despise the uninfluential and to treat with harshness the "little ones" of the kingdom, those who were weak and erring and always needing forgiveness. Our Lord therefore warns them that the little ones rather than the great ones are His care, and that provision is made in His kingdom not for those who need no forgiveness, not for those who can see only the faults and weaknesses of others, but for those who make constant demands on mercy.

But Peter, when he hears the precept that he must gain his brother by forgiving him his trespass, foresees the very probable result, that his brother thus forgiven will repeat his offence, and puts therefore the question whether some different treatment ought not then to be adopted. "How often," he says, "shall I forgive my brother?" He knew the Jewish rule: Forgive a first offence, forgive a second, a third—punish the fourth. And he seems to wish to meet at once the most liberal sentiments of his Master in expanding this common law to more than double its original measure: "Shall I forgive him till seven times?" But this question was framed in the very spirit of the old law of retaliation. By proposing any limit whatever to forgiveness, Peter showed that he still considered that to forgive was the exceptional thing, was to forego a right which must some time be reassumed, was not an eternal law of the kingdom but only a tentative measure which at any moment may be revoked; that underneath the forgiveness we extend to an erring brother there lies a right to revenge which we may at any time assert. This feeling wherever it exists shows that we are living with retaliation for the law, forgiveness for the exception. But Christ's law is, that forgiveness shall be unlimited: "I say not unto seven times, but until seventy times seven"— that is to say, an untold number of times. Seven was with the Jews the number of perfection,

When time has run through seven days, it begins again; the circle is complete. So that no expression could more forcibly convey the impression of endless, ever-renewed, eternal iteration than "seventy times seven."

The parable is added to illustrate the hatefulness of an unforgiving spirit. In it the Lord gibbets the implacable temper of the man who refuses to extend to others the forgiveness he himself needs. His own debt of something like two millions sterling indicates that he occupied a position of trust, and had exceptional opportunity of advancing his Lord's interests. And probably the magnitude of the debt was intended not merely to suggest the vastness of the liabilities of all men to God, but also to hint to the Apostles that men so closely allied to their Lord as they were, might possibly incur a greater debt than those in an inferior position had opportunity of incurring.

It may seem as if there were some inconsistency between the two parts of our Lord's directions regarding the treatment of an offending brother. In the parable and in His direct answer to Peter's question He speaks as if the sole duty of an injured person were to forgive. In the preceding verses He speaks as if much more were needful, and indeed He lays down the principles which have ever since governed, theoretically at least, ecclesiastical prosecutions.

An injured person is not to act as a strong healthy minded, good-natured man is very apt to act. He is not to say to himself, " What does it matter that so-and-so has called me 'cheat' or 'liar;' my character will outlive his attacks; what harm has he done save to himself by circulating slanders about me, or by taking me in to the extent of a few pounds? I am not going to dirty my hands or bother my head about such a poor creature." No doubt there are slight injuries of which this is the proper treatment. To notice them at all would be to make them of more importance than is wise. But this may be carried too far; and it is frequently carried too far by the easy-going, pleasant-tempered men who are so agreeable an element in society. There are, says our Lord, offences of which the proper treatment is to go to the offending party and remonstrate with him. There are few more disagreeable duties in life, but sometimes it is a duty. There are matters that come to your knowledge which you cannot pass by—you feel that if you do so, it is because of an element of cowardliness in your nature. Duty requires you to go to the offending party and endeavour to bring him to repentance.

But this treatment and all that follows it is in strict harmony with the injunction to forgive, for you are never required to forgive an impenitent person : but you are required—and this is, I think, a duty more difficult and more frequently neglected than even the duty of forgiveness—you are required to do all you can to bring to repentance the person who has injured you. To forgive the man who has wronged you, when he comes humbling himself, admitting he was wrong and heartily begging you to forgive him, in most actual cases makes no great call on Christian charity: but to go affectionately and without a spark of vindictive feeling to the man who has done you a wrong, and strive patiently to make it as plain to him as it is to yourself that he has done wrong, and so to do this as to win your brother—this seems to be about the highest reach of Christian virtue we are likely to meet in this present world.

There is another initial difficulty. Not only do we feel it almost impossible to forgive certain injuries, but some well-instructed Christian writers explicitly maintain that there are injuries which men ought not to forgive.* One who has done much to elevate the tone of modern literature, introduces the following lines in his most celebrated drama :

---

* On this point, see the remarkable chapter on Forgiveness, in "Ecce Homo," from which the thought of this paragraph is derived. The Author cites a modern novelist who makes one of his characters say: "There are some wrongs that no one ought to forgive, and I shall be a villain on the day I shake that man's hand."

> "Oh sirs, look round you lest you be deceived,
> Forgiveness may be spoken with the tongue,
> Forgiveness may be written with the pen,
> But think not that the parchment and mouth pardon
> Will e'er eject old hatreds from the heart.
> There's that betwixt you been men ne'er forget
> Till they forget themselves, till all's forgot,
> Till the deep sleep falls on them in that bed
> From which no morrow's mischief knocks them up."

It might seem then as if those who knew human life best agreed that there *is* a limitation which must be put to forgiveness, that there are injuries which no man can be expected to forgive or can forgive, that there are circumstances in which this rule of Christ's must be set aside.

Let us test this idea by a very simple instance. Some of the most thoroughly Christian and wise headmasters have been inclined to wink at fighting among their boys, taking care that it does not become too frequent nor go any serious length. And even the most forgiving and Christlike of parents is not altogether comfortable if his boy comes home from school and tells him that he was grossly insulted and struck by a boy somewhat bigger than himself, but that instead of defending himself he forgave the offender. Why then is the parent not quite comfortable, why would most parents be really more gratified to hear that their boy had fought a bigger boy, than that when struck he had turned the other cheek? Simply because most parents might have some suspicion that softness and cowardliness had as much to do with the turning of the other cheek as Christian feeling. If they had unmistakable proof of their boy's courage and manliness, if they were perfectly sure that fear was a quite unknown feeling to their boy, they would delight in his having forgiven insolence and ill-treatment. But unfortunately fear and a craven spirit are so much commoner than high spirit moderated by Christian temper, that wherever gross injuries are forgiven, we are apt to ascribe this apparently Christian conduct to that spirit which is at the very antipodes from the spirit of Christ. The parent does not think his boy *ought* not to forgive—nay, he is sure that is the highest and manliest, and to many boys the most difficult conduct—but until he is quite sure that in a given case the forgiveness has sprung not from a sham magnanimity thrown over a sneaking and feeble character, he is afraid to commend it.

So it is everywhere. There is *no* limitation to forgiveness; no injury so gross that it ought not to be forgiven. But there are injuries so gross that when men forgive them they are sure to be suspected of doing so from unworthy motives. So little is Christian feeling in its highest reaches and manifestations counted on, so little is it seen or even understood, that when a man forgives one who has deeply injured him, this forgiveness is apt to be ascribed to what is mean, and not to what is Christlike in the injured party. But wherever, as in the case of our Lord Himself, there is no question of the power to defeat or the courage to face one's enemies, wherever forgiveness can be ascribed only to a merciful spirit, there men do admire the disposition to forgive even the greatest of injuries.

The parable is intended to enforce the teaching of our Lord regarding forgiveness by exhibiting the unreasonableness and meanness and danger of an unforgiving spirit. The hatefulness of such a spirit is emphasized by two aggravating features:—

1. The unmerciful servant had himself required forgiveness and had just been forgiven.

2. The debt due to him was infinitesimally small when compared with the debt which had been remitted to him.

1. First, the man is not softened by the remission of his own great debt. He goes straight from the presence of his master who had forgiven him all his talents, and lays violent hands on one of his associates who happened to owe him a few shillings. Having just been forgiven, he might have been expected to remember, with humble and softened feeling, that there is a

better law than retaliation. He thought mercy a good thing so long as he was the object of it. So long as he was in the presence of a creditor he had much to say of the calamity of debt, a thousand reasons to urge for the exercise of patience, and a thousand excuses for wrongdoing. Five minutes after, in the presence of a debtor, there is to him no law in the world, but harsh and hasty exaction of dues. He is deaf to the reasons which had filled his own mouth immediately before, deaf to everything which was not a promise to pay, and that instantly.

This is no over-coloured picture. It is over-coloured neither as a representation of what naturally occurs in connection with pecuniary debts, nor as a picture of the treatment which sinners give to sinners like themselves. Men who begin to use the money which belongs to others, and to invest on their own account funds which either do not exist at all except in their own hopes, or which belong to others and are only passing through their hands, become deadened with surprising rapidity to all sense of the injury they do. If they prove bankrupt, it is much more their own inconvenience and loss they bewail than the wrong done to others. The enormous debtor of the parable betrayed no sense of shame, no feeling for his lord's loss, but only craven dread of slavery and personal suffering. No serious humility, no honest and thoughtful facing of the facts, no deep truthfulness have entered his spirit. He is ready to promise anything, if he can only escape present consequences.

This is a true picture of the temper in which we sometimes crave pardon. Our iniquities overtake us with a throng of painful and overwhelming consequences, and in terror we cry for forgiveness. But the distress of our own condition blinds us to the wrong we have done, and no true humiliation enters the spirit. Deadened by long self-indulgence to a sense of everything but what directly affects himself with pleasure or pain, the sinner has no thought of the deeper spiritual relations of his sin. He stupidly thinks God withholds punishment because he has made a foolish purpose of paying his dues by amending his ways. There is no deep contrition; no conscience-stricken yet joyful recognition of the relation he holds to God; no intense delight and glorying in a God capable of passing by such transgressions as his; no rising of the spirit to new attachments and new ideas; no "truth in the inward parts," but only a desire to escape, as selfish and as soft as was the desire to sin.

But the forgiving love of God, if it does not humble, hardens us. To carry an unhumbled, self-regarding spirit through such an experience gives the finishing touch to a dehumanizing selfishness. We have a key here to the conduct of those religious persons who act as if they meant to make up for their own deficiencies by charging others with theirs ; as if they supposed that the violent and unrelenting condemnation of those who offend them were the fittest exercise of their privilege as persons forgiven of God. The little taste of religion they have had seems to have soured their temper and hardened their heart. They would be more human had they no religion at all. Just as this man proposes to build up his credit again by scrupulously exacting every farthing that others owe him, so do those who have not been thoroughly humbled by God's forgiveness show their zeal in exposing and reproving the faults of others. So far from being softened and enlarged in spirit by their own experience of mercy, they grow more punctilious in their exactions, more cruel and stiff in their demeanour.

2. Second, the petty amount of the debt he exacts is set over against the enormity of that which had been remitted to himself. You might expect that a man who had been forgiven talents would have no heart to exact pence. You would suppose that one whose eye had been fixed on a kingdom's revenue would not know how to count farthings. There is something almost incredibly mean as well as savage in this man's quick remembrance of the few pence due to himself, while he so easily

dismisses from his mind the ten thousand talents due by him. But our incredulity gives way as we look at the facts which underlie the parable, and measure the debt we owe to God with the peccadilloes committed against ourselves, and which we are so slow to forget.

What are the offences which we feel it impossible to forgive, and which alienate us from one another? If other men do not serve us well and fulfil our expectations; if they do not throw themselves heartily into our work and perfectly accomplish what we entrusted to them, we have no forgiveness for them; they must go. Or some one has been so presumptuous as to differ from us, and has opposed the propagation of our opinions on some political, or theological, or practical matter. Or men patronise us, and make us feel insignificant; or they tell some damaging story about us; or they win the prize that we worked for, or succeed in getting possession of a little bit of property we coveted. Or has even some grand exceptional injury been been done you? has your whole life been darkened and altered and obstructed by the injustice or neglect or selfishness of some one, whose influence circumstances compel you to submit to? Is there some one whom you cannot think of but with a tumult in the blood and a passionate emotion? Take the injury that is most difficult for you to forgive, and measure it with that for which you yourself need to ask forgiveness of God, and say whether you ought to be implacable and resolved on revenge.

I suppose there are few persons who have not often sat and wondered why it is that they feel so little sense of obligation to God, and so little shame that their sins are sins against Him. It is so difficult for us to have any genuine shame before God, though so easy to feel it before men, that we are sometimes tempted to fancy that a sense of sin must after all be a fictitious feeling, and not a feeling which increases in intensity with soundness of mind and clearness of mental vision. Several considerations, however, combine to show that the representation given in the parable fairly apportions the comparative guilt of sinning against God and sinning against man. All our sins directly or indirectly touch God, while only a few touch any individual on earth. In the injuries done to yourself by other men you may be able to detect more malice, more intention to wound and injure than has entered into any sin you have committed against God. But then, what are the obligations which bind any man to your service compared with the obligations which bind you to God? For whom have you done, or for whom can you do, any portion of that which God daily does for you?

Debt is measured by obligation. There can be no debt where there has been no obligation. We are not equally bound to all. We are not bound to educate another man's children as we are bound to educate our own. We can have no debt to a shopkeeper from whom we have received nothing. And our debt to God is enormous because we have received from Him benefits deep as life itself, and are bound to Him in ways as varied as the manifestations of that life. We cannot sin against one another as we can sin against God. Just as the servant of the parable, in dealing with his lord, had intromissions with larger sums than he could touch in dealing with a fellow-servant, so in dealing with God we are lifted to relations unique in kind and of surpassing sacredness, and are involved in responsibilities of wider and deeper consequence than any that would otherwise attach to our life.

There ought, then, to be some proportion between our perception of the wrong done us and the wrong we do. If we so keenly feel the prick of a needle when inflicted on ourselves, we may be expected to consider with some compunction the gaping wounds we inflict on another. Is our shame for sin against God as intense and real as the blaze of indignation, or is it continuous and persistent as the slow-burning hate which an injury done to ourselves begets? In speaking of those who defraud or injure us we express our opinion of what wrongdoing deserves. Is our judgment as explicit, our feeling as strongly expressed in regard to our own transgressions? As strongly? But they ought to be a thousand times more vehement; there should be against ourselves an indignation such as no enemy of ours could excite against himself though his offences were many times aggravated. And what, after all, is our reputation, our happiness, our property, that we should make much wail about injury done to them? Our good name and our advancement in the world are no doubt much to ourselves, but they are of very little moment indeed to the world at large.

The fate of the unmerciful servant tells us in the plainest language that the mere cancelling of our guilt does not save us. It tells us that unless the forgiveness of God humbles us and begets within us a truly meek and loving spirit, we cannot be owned as His children. The best assurance that we are ourselves forgiven is the consciousness that the very spirit of the forgiving God is working in our own hearts towards others.

> "'Tis not enough to weep my sins,
> 'Tis but one step to heaven;
> When I am kind to others, then
> I know myself forgiven."

K

"He that revengeth shall find vengeance from the Lord, and He shall surely retain his sins. Forgive thy neighbour the hurt that he hath done unto thee, *so* shall thy sins also be forgiven when thou prayest. A man beareth hatred against another, and doth he seek pardon from the Lord? He showeth no mercy to a man who is like himself: and doth he ask forgiveness of his own sins?" (Ecclesiasticus xxviii. 1-4.) "If ye forgive not men their trespasses neither will your heavenly Father forgive your trespasses." If you are hard, unrelenting; always chiding; slow to recognise merit, quick to observe faults; admitting no excuse and making no allowances; cherishing ill-will; still feeling resentment on account of injuries done you ten years ago; if there are persons from whom you would if you could exact the uttermost farthing—then you have reason to fear for your own forgiveness. Can you humbly beseech God, and with tearful eyes look up to Him for pardon while you have your foot upon your brother's neck or your hand at his throat? The very fact that you are proud and unbending should itself convince you that you have never been humbled before a forgiving God. The very fact that you can be overbearing and exacting should prompt you to question most seriously whether you have in very truth let your heart be flooded with God's undeserved pardoning mercy. The very fact that in any relation of life you can carry yourself in a haughty, imperious, and unchastened manner should bid you ask whether in very truth you are at heart lowly before God as one who day by day needs His forbearance and pardon. Every bitter word you speak, every unmerciful, inconsiderate act you do, every relentless, cruel, exacting thought you have, casts suspicion on your Christianity, and makes it seem possible that your Master may yet have to mete to you with your own measure.

Thus then does the Lord lay down the law of unlimited forgiveness as a law of His kingdom. The kingdom or society He came to form, that new grouping and association of men which He means to be eternal, cannot be held together without the observance of this law. This is one of the essential laws of His kingdom. Men are to be held together and to work smoothly together not by external compulsion, not by a police agency, not by a criminal law of alarming severity—it seems ludicrous to speak of such forces in connection with an eternal and perfect society—but it is to be held together by the inward disposition of each member of it to forgive and be on terms of brotherly kindness with every other member.

We lose an immense deal of the power and practical benefit of Christ's teaching by refusing to look at things from His point of view, and to listen as cordially to what He says of His kingdom as to what He says of individuals. We are not perhaps too much but we are too exclusively taken up with the saving of our own souls. We neglect to consider that the Bible throughout takes to do with the Church and people of God, with the kingdom, and with the individual only as a member of the kingdom. It is not for the individual alone that Christ legislates. He does not point out a path by which one man by himself can attain to a solitary bliss; but He founds a kingdom, and lays down as its fundamental law the law of love, a law which shows us that our individual happiness and our individual perfection can only be won in fellowship with others, and by truly entering into the most enduring bonds with them. To unite us again individually to God, our Lord recognises as only half His work: to unite us to one another is as essential. Salvation consists not only in our being reconciled to God, but also in our being reconciled to men. When we attach ourselves to Christ we become members of a society, and can no longer live an isolated life. We must live for the body we belong to. Until we catch this *esprit de corps* we are poor Christians. The man who is content if he is sure his own soul is safe has great cause to believe it in danger; for there is no surer mark of a healthy Christian than his practical acknowledgment of the claims of other men and his interest in the kingdom to which he belongs.

But how are we to attain to that thoroughly healthy state of spirit to which it shall be natural to forgive until seventy times seven? This parable indicates that the most important step towards this is taken when we learn to accept God's forgiveness in a right spirit. The true way to a forgiving spirit is to be forgiven, to go back again and again to God, and count over our debt to Him. The man who thinks justly of his own wrong-doing has no heart to make much of the injuries done to himself. He always feels how much more he has been forgiven than he can ever be called upon to forgive. His soul gladdened, softened, and humbled by a sense of the great compassion that has remitted his great debt, loses all power to be harsh and damnatory.

We must therefore begin with the truth about ourselves. It is not required of us that we go out of our way to make an ostentatious display of our guilt, but it is requisite that we let the conviction of our great debt so sink into our minds that we shall go softly all the days of our life. It is required of us that we discover and recognise the truth about ourselves, and that we abide and walk in the truth and not in the unreal world of our own self-satisfied fancy. It is required of us that we have a character, and that this character be founded on and grow up out of God's forgiving grace. We need not proclaim to every man we meet the reason, but we must let all men see that we have a reason for loving-kindness, for humility, for gravity, for tender consideration of others, for every quality that banishes hatred from earth and welds men closer into one community.

VIII.

LABOURERS IN THE VINEYARD.

FIRST LAST AND LAST FIRST.

"For the kingdom of heaven is like unto a man that is an householder, which went out early in the morning to hire labourers into his vineyard. And when he had agreed with the labourers for a penny a day, he sent them into his vineyard. And he went out about the third hour, and saw others standing idle in the market-place, and said unto them; Go ye also into the vineyard, and whatsoever is right I will give you. And they went their way. Again he went out about the sixth and ninth hour, and did likewise. And about the eleventh hour he went out, and found others standing idle, and saith unto them, Why stand ye here all the day idle? They say unto him, Because no man hath hired us. He saith unto them, Go ye also into the vineyard; and whatsoever is right, that shall ye receive. So when even was come, the lord of the vineyard saith unto his steward, Call the labourers, and give them their hire, beginning from the last unto the first. And when they came that were hired about the eleventh hour, they received every man a penny. But when the first came, they supposed that they should have received more; and they likewise received every man a penny. And when they had received it, they murmured against the goodman of the house, saying, These last have wrought but one hour, and thou hast made them equal unto us, which have borne the burden and heat of the day. But he answered one of them, and said, Friend, I do thee no wrong: didst not thou agree with me for a penny? Take that thine is, and go thy way: I will give unto this last, even as unto thee. Is it not lawful for me to do what I will with mine own? Is thine eye evil, because I am good? So the last shall be first, and the first last: for many be called, but few chosen."—MATT. XX. 1-16.

LABOURERS IN THE VINEYARD.

FIRST LAST AND LAST FIRST.

MATT. xx. 1-16.

THE key to this parable is found in the question to which it was the answer, and in the circumstances which suggested that question. A young man of high character and still higher aspirations, but of unfortunately great wealth, had recognised in Jesus a teacher who in His own person and demeanour bore evidence that He understood how man could attain to the highest ideal. He accordingly introduced himself to our Lord as one who was bent upon achieving the highest human attainment, and who was only anxious to know what more could be done beyond what he had already accomplished. But on learning that for him the path to perfection lay through the abandonment of his great possessions, he felt that this was more than he could do, and turned away ashamed and wretched. As he passed out of sight, our Lord, sympathizing with the severity of his temptation, turned to His disciples, and with

His usual form of strong asseveration, said, "Verily I say unto you, that a rich man shall hardly enter into the kingdom of heaven."

When Peter saw how keenly the Lord appreciated the difficulty of giving up property and detaching oneself from familiar comforts and employments, he suggested that those who overcame this difficulty were peculiarly meritorious. "Behold," he says, "we have forsaken all and followed Thee: what shall we have therefore?" But in asking this question Peter betrayed precisely that disposition which most thoroughly vitiates all service of Christ, the disposition to bargain, to work for a clearly defined reward and not for the sake of the work itself and in generous trust in the justice and liberality of the Master. Peter had to all appearance made, so far as was possible in his circumstances, the very sacrifice which the rich young man had declined to make; but if a sacrifice is made merely for the sake of winning for oneself some greater gain, then it is no longer a sacrifice but a bargain. Love and trust are of the essence of sacrifice. Peter had left his home, his boat and fishing gear, and all the pleasant associations of the lake; he had torn himself up by the roots; but if he had done so not from simple love of Christ which found its ample reward in His company, but with a clear understanding that he would have a good return in kind for all he had given up, then he was perhaps premature in so complacently comparing himself with the rich young man. It is the motive which gives virtue to any sacrifice or service. The spirit which asks what compensation is to be made for every sacrifice, is self-regarding, mercenary, greedy, not generous, trustful, loving: it confounds two things diametrically different, bargain and sacrifice.

The Lord's answer to Peter's question is twofold. He first assures His followers that they shall have ample compensation for all present loss. Sharing with Him in work, they shall share in His reward. The results He works for shall be theirs as well as His. But having given them this assurance, He takes occasion to rebuke the disposition to bargain, the somewhat craven spirit that sought to be quite sure it would take no harm by following Him. And He warns them against comparing their sacrifices and services with those of other men, affirming that many who, like the apostles, were called at the very beginning of the Lord's ministry, and were first not only in point of time, but in eminence of service, and who might therefore seem sure of a conspicuous and exceptional reward, will after all be found no better off than those whose expectations have been extremely meagre. "Many shall be last that are first, and first that are last."

It was to illustrate this statement that the parable of the labourers in the vineyard was spoken. This is the point of its teaching to which all else is subordinate. The nature of the work in the vineyard and its exhausting toil; the unwearied compassion of the Lord of the vineyard, going out hour after hour to invite the unemployed; these and all other details are but the feathers of the arrow helping it to fly straight to its mark; but the point is, that those who were first hired were last paid and least paid, and this because the first-hired entered on their work in a bargaining spirit and merely for the sake of winning a calculated and stipulated remuneration, whereas the late-hired labourers did their work in faith, not knowing what they were to get, but sure they would not get less than they deserved.

The parable, then, is intended to show us the difference between work done in a bargaining spirit and work done in trust; between the reward given to work which in quantity may be very great but in motive is mercenary, and the reward given to work which in quantity may be very small, but in motive is sound. It directs attention to the fact that in estimating the value of work we must take into consideration not only the amount done or the time spent upon it, but the motive that has entered into it. It is this which God chiefly regards. One hour of trustful, humble service is of greater value to God than a life-time of calculating industry and self-regarding zeal. A gift that is reckoned by thousands of pounds; an ecclesiastical endowment that makes a noise through a whole generation; a busy, unflagging, obtrusive zeal which makes itself seen and felt throughout a whole land, these things make a great impression upon men—and it is well if they do not make a great impression on the parties themselves who do them and prompt them inwardly to say, "What shall we have therefor"—but they make no impression upon God unless animated by a really devoted spirit. While men are applauding the great workers who ostentatiously wipe the sweat from their brows and pant so that you can hear them across the whole field, God is regarding an unnoticed worker, who feels he is doing little, who is ashamed that any one should see his work, who bitterly regrets he can do no more, who could not name a coin small enough to pay him, but who is perfectly sure that the Master he serves is well worth serving. It is thus that the first become last and the last first.

That we are meant to see this difference of spirit in the labourers is obvious alike from the terms of their respective engagements, from the distribution of the wages, and from the temper shown by the last paid men.

1. First, the parable is careful to state that

those who were hired early in the day *made an agreement* to work for a stipulated sum. This sum was the usual day's wage of the period: a fair wage, which of itself was sufficient inducement to work. These men were in a condition to make their own terms. They ruled the market. At four or five in the morning the labourers in a hiring market have a keen sense of their own value, and are in no mood to sell themselves cheap. The masters and stewards have a very hard time of it as they are hooted from knot to knot of lusty fellows with the pride of the morning in their faces, and strive in vain to pick up labour at a reasonable figure. No man in the market at that hour engages without making his own terms, without saying what So-and-so offers, without knowing to a halfpenny what he will have, and striking hands with his hirer as his equal. The labourer means to make a good thing of it for himself; if he does not like the look of one steward he chooses another, if he thinks one master's pay too little he waits for a better offer. He is not going to work all day to oblige some neighbouring proprietor, he is going to work to make a good wage for himself. It's hot, hard, thirsty work, but it pays.

But in the evening the tables are turned. The masters now have it all their own way. It's no longer, "Will you give us more than So-and-so? what will you offer?" but "We'll leave that to you, sir; supper and a bed at the most is all we can expect. There's scarcely time to get to your place, but we'll hurry and do our best, if you'll have us at all." Possibly these men were the proudest in the morning, and missed their chance. Group after group of men has been detailed off at various hours, and now the shadows begin to lengthen; their pride gives place to hunger and anxious thoughts of the coming night. They are beginning to have gloomy thoughts of lying down in the darkness, with no food to refresh them, no roof to shelter, no promise of more work from an appreciative master, no pleasant talk and song with their comrades in the vintage. But as the day wears desolately away, and as now the hard taskmasters are heard on all sides beating down the wages of the jaded hirelings, there rises the considerate voice of this good and upright householder, "Go ye also into my vineyard, and whatsoever is *right*, that shall ye receive." In no condition to make a bargain, they most gladly trust themselves to one whose words have the ring of truth. They go, glad to get work on any terms; they go, not knowing what they are to get, but quite sure they are in good hands. They go humble, trusting, and grateful; the others went proud, self-confident, mercenary.

2. Secondly, the same difference in the spirit in which each set of labourers had entered on

their work is implied in the striking scene which ensued at the close of the day. Those who had barely got their work begun were *first* paid, and were paid a full day's wage. There must, of course, have been a reason for this; it was not mere caprice, but was the result and expression of some just idea. It could not be that these late-hired labourers had done as much in their one hour as the others in twelve; for the others, those who had worked the full day, are conscious of having done their work well. No hint is given that they were less skilful or less zealous than the late-hired men. We are thrown back, therefore, for the explanation on the hint given in the hiring, namely, that those who wrought merely for the sake of pay received the pay they looked for, while they who came to the vineyard conscious that they had wasted their day and not daring to stipulate for any definite wage, but leaving themselves confidently in the hands of a master they believed in, were gladdened by the unmerited reward of the fullest wage. The men who bargained were paid according to their bargain; the men who trusted got far more than they could have dared to bargain for.

The principle is more easily understood because we ourselves so commonly act upon it. The man who bargains and must have everything in black and white, and thus shows that in working for you it is himself he is looking after and seeking to profit, gets every penny he bargained for, but not a penny beyond; whereas the man who fears his work may not please you, but, if you wish it, will try and do his best, and says not a word about pay—to this man you give as much as you decently can, and always more than he is expecting. What you relish and reward, God also relishes and rewards. It is work done with some human feeling in it that you delight in. What you give out to be done at a certain rate you accept and pay for, but take no heed of him who does it. There is nothing personal between you. He does not work for you, but for his wage. His work may be most important and thoroughly well done, it may bear the mark of time and toil upon it, but it is the work of a hireling with whom you are quits when you pay him what he contracted to receive.

3. Thirdly, the same difference of spirit among the labourers is brought out in the envious and grudging temper of the first hired and last paid men. Peter must have felt himself gravely rebuked by the picture here drawn of the man who had listened to the first call of Christ, but who, after a full, honest day's work, was found to be possessed of a selfish, grudging spirit that filled him with discontent and envy. It was now plain that this early-hired labourer had little interest in the work, and that it was no

satisfaction to him to have been able to do twelve times as much as the last-hired labourer. He had the hireling's spirit, and had been longing for the shadow and counting his wages all day long. English sailors have been known to be filled with pity for their comrades whose ships only hove in sight in time to see the enemy's flag run down, or to fire the last shot in a long day's engagement. They have so pitied them for having no share in the excitement and glory of the day that they would willingly give them as a compensation their own pay and prize-money. And the true follower of Christ, who has listened to the earliest call of his Master and has revelled in the glory of serving Him throughout life, will from the bottom of his heart pity the man who has only late in life recognised the glory of the service, and has had barely time to pick up his tools when the dusk of evening falls upon him. It is impossible that a man whose chief desire was to advance his Master's work, should envy another labourer who had done much less than himself. The very fact that a man envies another his reward is enough of itself to convict him of self-seeking in his service.

The difference in the spirit of the workers which is thus brought out in the parable will be found, says our Lord, in the Church, and it will be attended with like results at the time of judgment and award. Here also "many that are first shall be last," not all, but many; so commonly will this be exemplified that there must be something in the nature of the case inducing it. Many who have done the largest works shall receive the smallest reward. Many first in man's esteem shall be last in God's reckoning. Many who have borne the burden and heat of the day, who have been conspicuous in the work of the church, whose names are identified with certain charities or philanthropic institutions will be rated below obscure individuals who have almost no work at all to point to. Many who have served longest in the Lord's vineyard have a consciousness that they are the great workers, which likens them to the self-complacent Peter rather than to the humble, trustful, self-ignoring spirit of the late-hired labourers. So, many who are most forward in the work of the Church and of the world are plainly animated by motives which are not above suspicion, that nothing is more obvious or more commonly remarked upon than that "many are called but few chosen." Many make trial of the work, and labour vigorously in it, but few have the purity of motive which gives them an abiding place, and wins the approval of Christ. And they especially are tempted to faultiness of motive who are first in work; they are impressed with their own consequence;

they find it difficult to avoid inwardly comparing themselves with those who waste their day; and moreover, many of those who live outwardly blameless and correct lives, and who abound in practical work, do so because they are originally of a calculating disposition.

But though many of the first, yet not all of them shall be last. This also we know to be true. Some at least of the best known workers in the vineyard, some who entered it early and never left it for an hour, some who scarcely once straightened their backs from toil, and dropped asleep as they came to the end of their task, knowing nothing but God's work their whole life through, have also wrought in no bargaining spirit, but passed as humble a judgment on their work as the last and least and lowest of their fellow-labourers on theirs. It is a thing that recalls the mind from thinking cynically and contemptuously of human nature to find how often the highest faculty, the most conspicuous and helpful gifts are used with absolute humility and lowliness, with scarcely one conscious thought that great good is being done. Happily there are some first who shall remain first; first at their work, and foremost in it; first in the field for amount and quality of work done, and yet first also in reward, because first in unaffected forgetfulness of self and pure devotedness to their

Master's interests, and to the work itself. As it is often the man who is first in the breach who least understands why men should praise him for courage, he himself having had no thought of danger; as the charitable man who has helped countless miserable creatures and made sacrifices which could not be hid, is distressed when his friends speak of making public recognition of his charity, so some who have most materially advanced the cause of Christ and of humanity are precisely those who think most shamefacedly of what they have done, and are unfeignedly astonished to hear they have been of any service, and cannot once connect the idea of reward with any toil they have undergone.

Again, as there are some first who remain first, so there are some last who remain last. Not all who enter the vineyard late enter it humbled. Not all who do little do it well. Mercenariness is not confined to those who have some small excuse for it. Even those who have wasted their life, and bring but the wreck of it into the kingdom, are sometimes possessed with a complacency and shamelessness that are astonishing to those who know their past history. To come to Christ late, and to come unhumbled, is the culminating exhibition of human complacency. To bring to the vineyard neither strength to labour nor purity of motive is the extreme of unprofitableness.

This parable, rightly read, gives no encouragement to late entrance into the Lord's service. To think of this service as that which we can add at any convenient time to the other work of life is to mistake it altogether. The service of Christ should cover the whole of life; and what is not done as a part of His work may in some respects as well not be done at all. All outside His vineyard is idleness. You may be busily, painfully engrossed in worldly business, and yet absolutely idle as to what conscience persistently reminds you is the one thing needful. Your life may be far through, as years go, but the main business of it not yet begun; your prospects always improving, yourselves no better than when you began. If there are those among you who feel this painfully enough, who keenly feel the vanity of life, who have tasted its distresses and disappointments, who know how little it all comes to, a few pleasures, a few excitements, one or two great changes, a great deal of dull labour, and a good many sorrows, and then the plunge into oblivion; if there are those who would welcome anything that would put a heart and a purpose into the whole, and lift every part of life up out of the low and despicable rut in which it for the most part moves, then why do you hesitate to respond when Christ says, "Why stand ye here all the day idle? Go ye into My vineyard, and what is right ye shall receive"? Do you not believe Him? Do you fancy that He will suffer you to spend yourself in what is despicable, and fruitless, and disappointing? Why waste your day? Why waste another hour of it, if there is real work to be done, if there is work of such importance to be done that He Himself left heaven to do it, if there is work to be done that the world needs, that men will be the better for, if there is the least opening for you to put your hand to what will stand God's inspection, why go on idling and frittering your one precious life away on what you yourself despise and are weary of?

Let us then examine ourselves in the light of this parable. Our Lord pointedly invites us to work for Him, to live for Him, and to do so in the assurance that whatsoever is right He will give. These labourers who went in faith got more than the men who had made what they considered a good bargain. In other words, you are as sure to be rewarded for every hour you spend in Christ's service as if you had His written bond and had made your own terms. If you had considered what you would like in return for anything you do for Him, and if you had stipulated for this, you would not thus have so much as you are sure to have by simply leaving it to Him. We need not concern ourselves about the future: we need not be mentally counting our wages; He would have us fall in love with the service, so that even though there were to be no reward at all, we should still choose it as the most honourable, the most useful, the most joyful way of spending our life, indeed as the one service which is perfect freedom, and satisfies our idea of what life should be. The slow, hesitating, suspicious person that thinks Christ wants to use him for some ends that are not the proper ends of human life, the foolish person that always feels as if Christ did not understand what it is that gives the truest relish to human life—such persons are not the labourers He desires. The bargaining spirit gets what it bargains for, but also gets His rebuke: the spirit that is too broken to bargain, too crushed and self-diffident to make terms, but can only go and work and trust, gets a reward that carries in it the hearty approval and encouragement of the Lord. Are you then in His vineyard at all, or are you still among the unhappy ones who cannot decide, or among those who have looked at the vineyard in the distance, and have fallen asleep in the market-place and are dreaming they are in it? or are you among those who eagerly watch for the reappearance of the Master, and as soon as He turns the corner of the street offer themselves to Him? He calls you now; He calls you every hour of the day. And if already in His service, are we among those who wish to know what they are to get or make by it? or do we leave all that to Him and enter His work because we are weary of idleness and sick at heart with hope deferred, or sore with the ill-usage we have received from other masters?

None of us, surely, dare push this parable aside and pass on into life without satisfying our conscience about this matter. Many of us are called. Many of us are in the vineyard, and have long been in it. We have borne, in a mild fashion, the burden and heat of the day. We have given money; we have spent a great deal of time; we have performed a number of worrying duties. And we mean to go on. Well, in what spirit have we laboured? Has it been to earn or maintain a reputation, or to make our influence felt? Has it been under a dim impression that such works and sacrifices are necessary in those who claim to be Christians? Have you rendered them as a kind of payment to enable you to maintain the feeling that you are Christ's people? Have you striven to help others mainly for the sake of doing yourself good, of helping out your own salvation, and keeping your own hands clean? Has your object been advantage to yourself, either future or present, spiritual or worldly? If so, you will have your penny, but the cordial approval of your master goes to others. You may say, Is it not right to aim at our own salvation, and do those good works which are needful for that purpose? Certainly it is right to save yourself, but it is better to save ten other people. It is he who loses sight of his own interests and forgets himself because he is so much taken up with the common work and the common good that finds he has won the highest reward.

Look, then, to your motives. See that it be pure love of the work and love of the Master that draw you to it. Actions are always within our own power. Hard work is always possible, and great sacrifices almost any man can make. It is the motive that is unattainable save by those whom Christ Himself has renewed.

IX.
THE TWO SONS.

" But what think ye? A certain man had two sons; and he came to the first, and said, Son, go work to day in my vineyard. He answered and said, I will not: but afterward he repented, and went. And he came to the second, and said likewise. And he answered and said, I go, sir: and went not. Whether of them twain did the will of his father? They say unto him, The first. Jesus saith unto them, Verily I say unto you, That the publicans and the harlots go into the kingdom of God before you. For John came unto you in the way of righteousness, and ye believed him not: but the publicans and the harlots believed him: and ye, when ye had seen it, repented not afterward, that ye might believe him."—MATT. xxi. 28-32.

THE TWO SONS.

MATT. xxi. 28-32.

THE three parables of which this is the first were spoken at one time, and that the most critical of our Lord's life. He had come to Jerusalem knowing the danger of doing so, but also persuaded that it was now high time to bring matters to an issue. He saw that things were now ripe for a public manifestation of Himself as the Christ. A career of obscure philanthropy in Galilee could no longer be pursued. The time was past for His laying His hand on the mouth of those who would have published His majesty and proclaimed their conviction that He was the Son of God. He goes to Jerusalem, that in the temple itself and before the chief priests and constituted authorities, He may again proclaim His own dignity, and be explicitly and finally received or rejected. Accordingly He makes it impossible for the authorities any longer to overlook His actions. They are compelled by the growing excitement of the people to appoint a deputation of their best men to wait upon Him. This deputation challenge His right to teach in this unlicensed way, and put to Him the testing question, "By what authority doest thou these things," no doubt with the expectation that He would claim Divine authority, and so give them a handle against Him. But our Lord declines to give any account of His authority further than what was manifest in His words and deeds themselves. If they could not see divine authority in the things themselves, if they did not feel that in His presence they were in the presence of God, they were not likely to see or to feel the Divine presence merely because He said it was there.

It is astonishing with what persistency numbers of persons continue to make the demand of these priests, and put themselves in the condition our Lord condemns. They will not accept a thing as Divine because it has the attributes of Divinity attaching to it, but they ask for further evidence. They will not accept a teacher as inspired, because of the truth he utters, but ask for an authority external to himself, and over and above his teaching, which shall guarantee it to them. They will not bow before Christ Himself, because their whole nature finds in Him the highest and best they know; but, like these ignorantly dishonest priests, they ask for His authority. They ask for a guarantee outside of Himself which shall warrant them in trusting Him, as if there could be any possible guarantee so perfect as the actual moral supremacy they feel Him to possess. That man's faith is resting on a very precarious foundation who believes not because the truth itself has laid hold upon his conscience, but because he is yielding to authority; who accepts Christ, not because he finds in Christ the true Lord of His spirit, but because the claims of Christ are established by what is external to His person.

Jesus, however, is not content merely to evade their entangling question. He turns their assault against themselves, and so leads the conversation that they are compelled to utter their own condemnation in presence of the multitude. The parable is too plain-spoken to be evaded. They cannot deny that the satisfactory Son is not the one who professes great respect for His father's authority, while he does only what pleases himself, but the one who does his father's bidding, even though he has at first disowned His authority. They are compelled, that is, to own that a mere bowing to God's authority and professing that they attach great weight to it is of no account in God's sight unless it be accompanied by an actual doing of the things He enjoins. John came to you, our Lord says to the priests and elders, in the way of righteousness, enjoining the works that belong to the kingdom of God, setting clear before your conscience the duties actually incumbent on you.

You felt he was God's messenger, the words he spoke proved him to be so; the holy conduct he enforced compelled you inwardly to own him a messenger of God to you; you dare not now in the presence of these people deny that he was from God. Why then did you not do his bidding? He was God's messenger, he told you plainly who the Christ was, and yet you believed him not. You refused to work the work of God peculiar to your time and office, the work of acknowledging and believing in the Son of God, witnessed by John whom ye yourselves know to be a true witness. You come now and ask Me for my authority as if, were you convinced it was Divine, you would gladly yield to it; as if you were anxious to know God's will, as if there were on your lips constantly the "I go, sir," of this Son, whereas already it has been made clear to your own conscience what God would have you do regarding Me, and yet you obey Him not. These publicans and harlots whom you despise and loathe are in the kingdom of God while you are outside; for bad as they were and daringly as they had disowned God's authority, and little profession of belief in God as they made, they yet repented when John proclaimed the coming kingdom, and have believed in and submitted to the King.

These men were thus unceremoniously dealt with by our Lord because they were false.

THE TWO SONS.

They may not have clearly seen that they were false, but they were so. They were false because they professed to be anxious for additional evidence regarding Christ, while already they had sufficient evidence. They were resisting the light already shed into their conscience, and yet professed a desire for further light. And probably in no age of the world's history have there been so many in their state of mind as in our own. There is a very general misapprehension as to the amount and kind of evidence that may reasonably be demanded in favour of Christ's claims, and also as to the manner in which the evidence may be expected to find entrance into the mind and produce conviction. And it is certain that unless we use the light we have and follow it, we are not likely to reach fuller light. If we are at present sure that at any rate the moral teaching of Christ is healthy, let us practise that teaching; for, if we do not, we reject the aid which more than any other is likely to bring us to Christ's own point of view, and to open our sympathies with His purpose and to enlighten us regarding His whole position.

The application of the parable, then, to those to whom our Lord was speaking could not be misunderstood. The first son—the man who at first said he would not go but afterwards repented and went—was the representative of the publicans and harlots. They had openly asserted their unwillingness to work for God: they had made no professions of obedience, they had decidedly turned their backs on everything good. They had lived in open sin, and were not surprised that men should denounce them as hopelessly corrupt. The lad that plainly told his father he was not going to the vineyard but meant to have a holiday with his boon companions would not have been more astonished to be called a dutiful and obedient son, than these publicans and harlots would have been had any one addressed them as good and godly people. They knew they were doing wrong: they were conscious of their wickedness. But John's preaching went to their hearts, because he assured them that even for them there was an open gate into the kingdom of God. They repented because they were assured that for them there was place for repentance and a way back to purity of conscience, to holiness of life, to God.

The priests and elders, the men who represented all that was respectable and religious in the country, were depicted in the second son who promptly said he would go and work for his father, but did not do so. This son gives his answer in the one word "I," as if he meant, "Oh! you need have no doubt about me. I am ready. I am at your service. My brother is a shameless fellow, but as for me you have only to command me." This son takes it for granted he is the dutiful son; he puts no pressure on himself to secure obedience; he is conscious of no necessity to guard against temptations to forgetfulness, to indolence, to selfishness. He takes for granted that no deficiency will be found in him, and his complacency is his ruin. We all know this kind of man: the tradesman to whom you give elaborate instructions, and who assures you he will send you an article precisely to your mind, but actually sends you what is quite useless for your purposes; the friend who bids you leave the matter to him, but who has no sooner turned the corner of the street than he meets some one whose conversation puts you and your affairs clean out of his mind. If promising had been all that was wanted, no community could have been more godly than Jerusalem. These priests and elders spent their lives in professing to be God's people. Their day was filled with religious services. They had no secular business at all; they were identified with religion; their whole life was a proclamation that they were God's servants, and a profession of their willingness to obey. And yet they failed to do the one thing they were there to do. They heard John's teaching, they knew it was the voice of God, but they refused to prepare their hearts and understandings, as he taught them, that they might recognise Christ. The one thing that John commanded them to do, to prepare for and receive the King, they failed to do. Their whole profession collapsed like a burst bubble; they were proved to be shams, to be dealing in mere words with no idea of realities.

It is natural to suppose that the religious world will in every generation present similar phenomena. It requires no exceptional discernment to see that in our own day the spiritual condition of these priests and elders is abundantly reproduced. There are many now whose life is in great part devoted to various ways of declaring a willingness to serve God, but whose life is also marked by disobedience. If you listen to what these persons say you would fancy they were God's most industrious servants; if you look at what they do you find nothing done for God at all, or that their own peculiar and chief duty is neglected. Every person, therefore, who is conscious that he resembles this son in professing a willingness to do God's will, should consider whether he does not also resemble him in leaving that will undone. We seem to be anxious to discover what God would have us do. We read His word—we go where we hear it explained and enforced—we are rather proud of our exceptional knowledge of its meaning—we seem to set great value on any hand that will point out the way, on any voice that will say to us: There, that is the work for you.

But does not this forwardness in hearing what God's will is sometimes take the place of our doing it? Do we not sometimes mistake our zeal in hearing good counsel about spiritual things for a zeal in God's service? Is not our knowledge, or our pious feeling, or our known sympathy with religion, allowed to stand for actual work done? Are we not sometimes as satisfied with ourselves when we have seen clearly the reasonableness and desirableness of serving God, and when we have felt some desire to serve Him, as if we had, in fact, made a sacrifice in our business for the sake of righteousness? We congratulate ourselves on feeling well-disposed, we complacently number ourselves among God's people, we think with satisfaction of our clear and moving views of Christ's work; and when all these clear views and pious feelings have passed away without any result in the shape of work done, we still congratulate ourselves on having cherished them. There may be some doubt about our morality, but there can be none about our religion. Men may not be quite sure how far they can trust us in a business transaction; our influence at home may not be of the best kind; but no one can have any doubt that if the religious men of the city were convened our name would appear among the invited.

Let us then deal honestly with ourselves, and wipe off the reproach of promising without performing, and of staying among the mere preliminaries of obedience. God has desired us not only to think right, to cherish certain feelings, to maintain certain observances, but He has enjoined all those things as helps and incentives to the doing of His will. He has said to each of us, "Go, work." His call comes to us in this form. If you have any connection with God at all, He has said to you, "Go, work." And it is a poor reason, surely, to offer for our not working, that we have seen most clearly the reasons for working, and that no one has been more ready to promise obedience. Which of you, being a parent, would not stand amazed, if, when you challenged your child for not doing what you had told him, he were to say in excuse, "But I promised to do it; I know that I ought to have done it." Would you not fear that some strange obliquity of moral vision had affected your child; and would you not fear lest a child who could offer so utterly unreasonable an excuse might fall into the most flagrant and enormous vices?

The question, then, is, What have you *done*? The passer-by who saw the one son stripped and hard at work under the sun among the vines, while the other lounged simperingly on the road telling people what an admirable man his father was, and what a pleasure it was to work for him, and how much he hoped the vintage would be abundant—I say, the passer-by would have not the slightest difficulty in forming a judgment of the two sons. Would he that has noted your habits—and many have noted your habits—feel quite sure you were God's obedient son? Would he think it absurd to ask whether you had *said* you would obey, having the far better proof of an obedient spirit, that you were actually obeying? So judge yourself. Do not believe in your purpose to serve God better until you do serve Him better. Give no credit to yourself for anything which is not actually accomplished. Do not let us be always speaking of endeavours, and hopes, and intentions, and struggles, and convictions of what is right, but let us at last *do* God's will.

The other son bluntly refused at first to go and do his father's bidding. His father had addressed to him a most reasonable request, and applied to him an epithet much more endearing than our word "Son;" but he is answered with a harsh, surly refusal. There is no attempt made by the son to excuse himself or soften the refusal; no mention of previous engagements, private business of his own, or necessary duties elsewhere. He is unfeeling and wantonly rude, as well as disobedient. He represents, therefore, those who are rather forward in their repudiation of God's authority. So far from desiring to be considered godly, they rather affect a deeper, more resolute ungodliness than they feel, a more vicious wickedness than belongs to them. They flaunt their opposition to all that is Christian.

Such persons are frequently the subjects of a peculiar delusion. Being themselves quite honest and open in their ungodliness, they profess and cultivate a special abhorrence of hypocrisy. No character is so contemptible in their eyes as that which pretends to grace, and thus loses the pleasure both of sin and of holiness; and amidst all their enjoyments there are few greater than that which proceeds from the unmasking of some professed Christian. They seem to think hypocrisy the crowning sin; and so zealously do they cultivate their skill in detecting it that they become blind to every other. Like well-trained hounds, they know no game but what they are trained to hunt. And thus they actually glide into the belief that because they are not hypocrites, they are not in a dangerous position. But if a man is going to destruction, it is, after all, a poor consolation that he is doing so with his eyes open. Is it not time for a man to bethink himself, when he finds matter for self-gratulation in the fact that he does not make the smallest profession of serving God or of seeking to be saved? You are honest in refusing to assume a character you do not possess, but are you wise to refuse the real attainment of that character? You are honest in seeking to be known for what you are, but are you wise to be what you are? Could you not be equally honest were you nearer to God and liker Him? It will not stand you in the day when God takes account of His servants to say that you never professed to serve Him.

But the whole history of this first son is not that he refused to labour for his father; he afterwards repented and went. Perhaps the hurt look of his father had shot some compunction into his soul. Perhaps the very roughness of his own voice had startled him, and suddenly revealed to him how far he had gone in sin, and how fast his heart was hardening. Perhaps the weary gait of his aged and unassisted father, his feeble efforts to accomplish tasks that required younger sinews than his, his evidently heart-broken and listless and mechanical way of setting about the work—perhaps this smote the young man's heart as he lay sunning himself in indolence, and recalled old days when he was happy with his father, and went to carry the tools he was too young to use; and the old feelings of filial affection rose again within him, —he repented and went to the vineyard.

Are there none who know that it is time for them to follow this youth's example; none who are conscious they have not done their duty towards God; who have made no pretence even of doing God's will, but have persistently shut their eyes to His love, denied His claims, and despised His commandment? Do you feel no compunction? Are you worse than even those publicans and harlots who no sooner learned there was forgiveness and a clean life for them than they eagerly sought God? Do you prefer a life every hour of which pains and grieves your heavenly Father, and a life which in itself is condemned by God and man; do you prefer a life which in your sober moments you cannot yourself approve, and which lacks all tenderness towards God and all truth and purity, to a life which God Himself calls you to as worthy of you and as the beginning of never-ending blessedness? Were it possible for God to call you by name and from His unseen dwelling this moment to break silence and call you to work for Him, were He to tell you of His love for you and to invite you to turn to Him, would you refuse Him, *could* you refuse Him? Does He not then summon you now? Does He not do even more than this? Does He not speak within your own heart, and cause you to feel it were well and wise to meet with humble welcome all His overtures? Can you rest under the stigma of a hard-heartedness that cannot be moved by infinite tenderness? Can you rest content to turn away to your own poor private employments and ways while God offers you that which will make your whole work and your whole life true?

As a whole, this parable shows us how God is served by men, and shows us especially that though there are greater and less degrees of disobedience and impenitence, there is no such thing as consistent uniform obedience. The best that God gets from earth is the obedience of repentance. Men must still, each for himself, try their own way, and only when this is found to be quite foolish and hurtful and hopeless, do they try God's way. No one can take God's word for it that such and such are the things to be done; such and such others to be avoided. We must for ourselves know good and evil, we must be as gods making choice between the good that sin brings and its evil, and if then God's judgment about sin tallies with our own, we accept it. Such a thing as simple, perpetual acceptance of God's commands from first to last is not to be found; and repentance, though certainly to be rejoiced over, is, after all, only the second best thing. Apology, however sincere, is at all times a very poor substitute for conduct that needs none.* And yet you will

* So John Foster in his " Lectures."

often see that a man considers that a graceful apology, whether to God or men, more than repairs the wrong he has done.

Let us then be on our guard lest even our repentance be sin, and our humiliation tainted with pride. When we come to God with apology for neglect of duty, we are often as proud of having insight enough to see deeply into the evil of our hearts as we are humbled by a sense of the wrong we have done in omitting whole years of service. We seem to be more worthy of praise for discovering the sinfulness of a past action than of blame for committing it. We are secretly flattered by finding that we are taking our place among those who have a fine discernment of the higher duties of the Christian life and of the secret and subtle iniquities of the human heart, and when we confess these, it is with less shame than complacency. Through all our confession there is running a silent, "I thank Thee, Lord, that I am not as other men, who could not confess such sins as I am confessing, because they are still down among the glaring and immoral wickednesses, and have not so much as thought of those duties that I have been striving after." It is, no doubt, right to be convinced we have been wrong, it is right to turn in to God's vineyard, even though it be after refusing to do so, but that complacency should mingle with our repentance is surely a triumph of duplicity. To make our very confession of total unprofitableness matter of self-gratulation is surely the extreme of even religious self-deception.

But if we carry anything at all with us from this parable, it must be this: How greatly our knowledge is in excess of our action. Our Lord easily elicited from these persons an unqualified condemnation of conduct which precisely represented their own. They held in their minds principles which, had they only been applied to their own conduct, would have made them very different men. This reproach never passes from the world: all of us know more than we practise. In the best of us there lies unused a large amount of instructive, stimulating, consolatory knowledge. The worst regulated life, the conduct which is most shameful and hurtful, is frequently that of a thoroughly intelligent and well-instructed person. In the mind of the most careless among us there is held truth enough to save the world, and principles which, if only applied, would form an unblemished character. And which of us, when we recount and condemn the faults of others, does not show an intelligence and a zeal for virtue of which there is small sign in some parts of our own life?

The question which this parable suggests is not, what do you know? but, what are you doing? not, have you acknowledged the righteousness of God's demands? have you seen that it is good for you to obey? do you own and constantly profess that you are His servants? but, have you *done* what God has given to you to do? God has commanded you to love Him with all your heart and strength; you know you ought, but have you done it? He has told you that this especially is the work of God, that you believe on Him whom he hath sent; have you done it? He calls you to work for Him, to consider what you can do to forward what is good, to set before you as your aim in life not advantage of any kind to yourself, but righteousness in yourself and in others. Do not despair of doing something useful; there are ways in which you can be helpful. These publicans and harlots might well have thought there was no room for them to do good in the community, and that their tastes were such that they could never love purity and truth and unselfishness. You may feel the same. You may feel that if you do the external duty you yet have no love for it, and you cannot bear to look forward to a life in which at every step you will require to put compulsion on yourself to do so. But such will not be the case. Do the duty, and the spirit will come. Obey God, and you will learn to love Him. Compel yourself to all duties now, and soon you will like the duties that are now distasteful. The man that is drawn out of the water half-drowned can only be restored by artificial respiration, but, if this is persevered in, the natural breathing at last begins, and the functions of healthy, unforced respiration supersede the artificial means. And thus God educates us to ease and naturalness in all duty. Under cover of the outward conduct, the new spirit grows and grows to such strength that at last it maintains the outward conduct as its natural fruit.

X.
THE WICKED HUSBANDMEN.

"*Hear another parable: There was a certain householder, which planted a vineyard, and hedged it round about, and digged a winepress in it, and built a tower, and let it out to husbandmen, and went into a far country: and when the time of the fruit drew near, he sent his servants to the husbandmen, that they might receive the fruits of it. And the husbandmen took his servants, and beat one, and killed another, and stoned another. Again, he sent other servants more than the first: and they did unto them likewise. But last of all he sent unto them his son, saying, They will reverence my son. But when the husbandmen saw the son, they said among themselves, This is the heir; come, let us kill him, and let us seize on his inheritance. And they caught him, and cast him out of the vineyard, and slew him. When the lord therefore of the vineyard cometh, what will he do unto those husbandmen? They say unto him, He will miserably destroy those wicked men, and will let out his vineyard unto other husbandmen, which shall render him the fruits in their seasons. Jesus saith unto them, Did ye never read in the scriptures, The stone which the builders rejected, the same is become the head of the corner: this is the Lord's doing, and it is marvellous in our eyes? Therefore say I unto you, The kingdom of God shall be taken from you, and given to a nation bringing forth the fruits thereof. And whosoever shall fall on this stone shall be broken: but on whomsoever it shall fall, it will grind him to powder. And when the chief priests and Pharisees had heard his parables, they perceived that he spake of them.*"— MATT. xxi. 33-45.

THE WICKED HUSBANDMEN.

Matt. xxi. 33-45.

"HEAR another parable," says our Lord to these ecclesiastical dignitaries who were probably feeling that they had heard quite enough already. Their dignity, they felt, was suffering in the eyes of the mob, who could not fail to see that the tables had been turned against them, and who rarely conceal the rough relish they have in contemplating the discomfiture of pompous ignorance and sanctimonious arrogance. If there flew round the circle none of those jeering remarks or smart personal hits which would inevitably have been elicited from an English crowd, there would not be wanting significant nods and satisfied smiles which would show with equal clearness to the priests and elders that in seeking to expose the pretensions of Jesus they had only exposed themselves. Their falseness in disguising their reluctance to accept Jesus as the Christ under pretence of seeking further evidence, was with a wonderful facility laid bare to all. They stood convicted of refusing to accept the testimony of one whom they dared not deny to be from God. They stood convicted of having incapacitated themselves for recognising the divine in Jesus. But theirs is not the guilt of the common unbeliever; it was not merely their personal duty and interest to keep themselves awake to the divine by righteousness of life, it was their official duty as well. It was the duty for which their office existed. They must therefore be shown up as men who are hollow shams, who are complacently maintaining their official dignity and the routine and forms of their office, while they are wholly oblivious of its one great object. They are worse than useless. They are as agents whom a man has appointed to manage his business or his property for him, and who use their position for embezzling the entire proceeds, and enriching themselves at his expense.

The parabolic dress under which this warning or judgment is carried home to them is a very thin veil, through which no one could fail to discern the living truth. The liberally cared-for vineyard, furnished with every advantage to facilitate productiveness, was of course Israel, hedged off from the outlying and less cared for fields of heathenism, and furnished with all that goes to fructify human nature. As God had long since declared, nothing that could be done had been left undone. As many men will go to any expense in improving their property, trying new methods, providing the best implements, taking a pride in having every road and fence in good repair, so everything had been done in Israel that could be expected to fertilize human nature. A small section of humanity had been railed off, and the experiment was made that it might be seen to what a pitch of productiveness this most fruitful of God's plants could be brought. A family or race of men was chosen and set apart for the very purpose of receiving every advantage which could help men to produce the proper fruit of man; to maintain a vigorous, healthy life, and to yield results which might seem to justify the care spent on them. There was to be a nursery of virtue, where any one would only have to look in order to see what proper cultivation could effect. Here it was to be shown that barbarism, degradation, violence, lust, and idolatry were not the proper fruit of human nature. In this garden man was to receive every possible aid and inducement to development and productiveness: nothing was wanting which could win men to holiness, nothing which could enlarge, purify, fertilize human nature.

And what was the result? The result was that which every reformatory in the country gives, namely, that human nature in the abstract is one thing; in the concrete, in the individual, another; that as some soils simply absorb all that you can put into them and give no sign, so do most men simply absorb all manner of inducements, counsels, warnings, aids, and bring forth nothing serviceable to God or man. Even persons professing religion are quite contented, nay, even think they are making vast attainment and thriving magnificently, when they are merely receiving, and doing nothing or little. They measure themselves by the care God is spending on them, not by the fruit they are yielding; by the amount of instruction they have received and retain, not by the use they have made of it; by the grace spent upon them, and not by the results. In short, they make the blunder which subverts the whole of religion, of turning means into ends.

But in this parable it is not the plants that are censured for barrenness, but the keepers of the vineyard that are condemned for unfaithfulness to the owner. The fruit borne, whether more or less than common, was intercepted by the husbandmen. They used their position solely for their own advantage. That is to say, the priests and elders of the Jews had fallen into the common snare of ecclesiastical leaders, and had used the dignity and advantageous position of their office for their own behoof, and had failed to remember that they had it only as

God's servants. The religious leader is quite as liable as the political or military leader to be led by a desire for glory, applause, notoriety, distinction, power. And the Church is quite as open a field for the exercise and manifestation of such unworthy motives as the State is.* The Church, being a society of men, must be managed by the usual methods, which all societies of men adopt. There must be combination, contrivance, adjustment, discussion, laws and regulations. The Church in its outward system and movements must be wrought by the same machinery as other large associations use. And it is notorious that the mere working of this machinery requires no spiritual faculty in the persons who manage it. It calls into exercise a certain class of gifts and faculties, certain talents and qualities which are eminently serviceable, but which may equally be exercised for the State or for the Church, for the world or for God. The political leader who negotiates with foreign powers, who foresees calamity and has skill to avert it, who can control large bodies of men and keep vast organizations in noiseless motion, may exercise these great gifts either for his country and his God, or merely for the sake of making or maintaining his reputation as the most influential man of his generation. And

* See the late Canon Mozley's Sermon on "The Reversal of Human Judgment."

the ecclesiastic who has very much the same kind of work to do, feeling the pulse of the theological and ecclesiastical world, making out through the distorting haze of public report and opinion what are the facts of a case and what is best to be done in it, and talking over to his view large bodies of men—this man, like the politician, may be serving his God, or he may be serving himself. Success may be the idol of the one as truly as of the other. To have a large religious following and wide influence in the Church may be as thoroughly selfish and worldly a desire as to be at the head of a strong political party. It is not the sphere in which one's work is done that proves its spirituality or worldliness; neither is it always the nature of the work that is done, but the motive that tests whether it is spiritual or worldly. These priests and elders had not escaped the snare into which their predecessors had fallen, and to which all their successors are exposed. They had used their position to attract applause to themselves, or to make their influence felt in the community, or to win for themselves a name as defenders of the faith.

Another and still more insidious form of the same temptation it may be worth while to notice. It is that temptation to which our Lord alluded when He censured this same class of persons for their zeal in proselytizing. But why so? Is not zeal in propagating religion a good thing? If these foremost men in the Jewish Church compassed sea and land to make one proselyte, is this not that very missionary zeal which the Jews are upbraided for wanting, and the modern Church prides itself on possessing? Is evangelistic fervour in the nineteenth century a thing to applaud, while the same fervour in the first is to be condemned? or what was it in these men's zeal that so roused our Lord's indignation? It was that same element which so often still taints zeal for the propagation of religious truth—the desire rather to bring men over to my way of thinking and so to strengthen my own position, than to bring them to the truth. My way of thinking may be the truth, or may, at least, be much nearer it than the opinions held by others, and for them it may be a good thing to be brought over to my views; but for myself it is a bad thing and the mere strengthening of a selfish craving, if I seek to propagate my opinions rather because they are mine than because they are the truth. And how wide-spreading and deep-reaching an evil this is, those well know who have observed religious controversy and seen how dangerously near propagandism lies to persecution. The zeal that proceeds from a loving consideration for others does not, when resisted, darken into violence and ferocity. The mother seeking to persuade her son does not become fierce when opposed, but only increasingly tender and pitifully gentle. The zeal for truth that storms at opposition and becomes bitter and fierce when contradicted, you may, therefore, recognise as springing from a desire rather to have one's own wisdom and one's own influence acknowledged than from either deep love for others or deep regard for the truth as the truth.

But to return—the implied and slightly disguised condemnation of the parable our Lord proceeds to enforce in an explicit form. The truth which had been sheathed in the parable He thrusts home now with naked point. "The kingdom of God shall be taken from you and given to a nation bringing forth the fruits thereof." And this warning is grounded not on a parable, which they might have affected to despise, but on a passage of the very Scriptures they professed to be the guardians of. There had been the warning before their eyes, read by them, sung by them at their festivals, carefully treasured in their memories; and yet, like us all, they had so little penetrated to its sense, had so little thought out its meaning and possible application, had looked upon it so much as a dead letter and so little as alive for them and for all men, that our Lord has yet to ask them: "Did ye never read in the Scriptures, The stone which the builders rejected is become the head of the corner?" Is not this stone the same as the heir sent by the lord of the vineyard? Are not ye now in danger of fulfilling the prophecy ye know so well? Are you not about to reject and cast contempt on one whom in your souls you know to be worthy of far other treatment?

The careful reader of this conversation will be struck with two points in it—first, that Jesus claims to be the heir of God; in other words, He deliberately sets himself on a wholly different level from the other prophets—high above Isaiah, Elijah, nay, even high above Moses himself. They were all servants; He is in quite a different relation to the proprietor, that is, to God. He is the Son and Heir; in acting for God He acts for Himself. It is because the vinedressers identify Him with the owner that they have a hope of gaining possession of the vineyard by killing the heir. To kill a mere servant would have served no such purpose; another servant can always be appointed; however high his office and title, another can always be raised, and equal authority can be delegated to him; but there is no other son. It is nature and relationship, not mere official dignity, that underlies this title and that is implied in the parable.

But the second point is even more worthy of remark. Our Lord implies that this was known by these Jewish leaders. Their condemnation was, that knowing Him to be the Son of God, they slew Him. Peter, indeed, apologetically says that they would not have slain Him had they known He was the Lord of glory. It may have been so in some instances; and, no doubt, had they allowed the fact to stand clear before their minds, had they given free course to it and weight to it, they could not have done what they did. Still, as the parable shows, it was just because they knew this was the heir that they were so eager to remove Him. Their state of mind is perfectly intelligible and very common. There lay latent in them a deep consciousness which they would not allow to become distinct and influential. They had a conviction that Jesus was the Christ, but they would not let their mind dwell upon it. There are few of us who have not such buried convictions, few of us who do not leave out of sight thoughts which, if allowed influence, would urge us to unwelcome action. There are thousands who have a haunting suspicion that Jesus deserves a very different kind of recognition from that which they give Him. Is there not lying in the mind of some of you half-formed thoughts about Jesus, possible if not actual convictions, which if you carefully thought them out would lead you to take up a different and much more satisfactory attitude towards Him?

And if there are those who feel that things should be plainer, that the majesty of Christ should be so borne in upon the soul that all would yield to Him, this is natural; but it is to overlook the fundamental fact that room must be left for freedom of choice and the exercise of judgment. The fact is, that the rejection of Christ by so many is one of the proofs that He is Divine. It is worldly worth that is acknowledged by all, and worldly blessings that are universally accepted. The higher the blessing, the fewer accept it. All wish plenty to eat, a minority value good education, a few seek the kingdom of God. And so our Lord here points out that it had long been foreseen that when He came He would be rejected. In reply to those questioners who ask how He can allow the Hosanna Psalm to be applied to Him by the people, He takes this very psalm, and out of it proves to the authorities that their very resistance and rejection of Him is the proof that He is what the crowd were affirming Him to be—the Messiah, the Son and Heir of God, the Stone despised of the builders, but chosen of God. Rejection by the builders was one of the marks by which the foundation chosen by God was to be identified. Truth is often more convincingly exhibited by the opposition of a certain class of men. It is not discredited by their opposition; but a *primâ facie* point in its favour is that they do not receive it. And, certainly, had the claims of Jesus been accepted by these dried-up formal traditionalists we should have had some cause for doubt.

Abandoning the figure used in the parable, our Lord makes use of a new figure to complete the warning. He speaks of two possible contingencies—"Whosoever shall fall on this stone shall be broken"—this had been declared by Isaiah—"but on whomsoever it shall fall, it will grind him to powder," this figure had been familiarized by Daniel's use of it. The stone which lies ready hewn and suitable for the best part of a building may inflict severe injury on the builder, either by his carelessly stumbling upon it, falling from a height upon it, and so getting himself bruised and broken; or it may fall from a height upon him, in which case it is certain death.

The first case is that in which Christ is a stone of stumbling to those to whom He is presented. God lays this stone everywhere in our way that we may build upon it or set it high in the place of honour, and we cannot simply walk on as if God had done no such thing. Whatever else Christ is, He is substantial, a reality as solid as the stone against which your foot is jarred. To make as if He were not, and to pass on untouched and unchanged, is impossible. If we attempt to do so, ignoring that the stone is there, we stumble and fall and injure ourselves. The foundation stone becomes a stone of offence. Every one who hears the gospel, every one in whose path Christ is laid, is either the better or the worse for it. The gospel once heard is "henceforward a perpetual element in the whole condition, character, and destiny of the hearer." No man who has heard can be as if he had not. Though he may wish to pass on as if he had not seen Christ at all, he is not the same man as he was before, his spiritual condition is altered, possibilities have dawned upon his mind, openings into regions which are new and otherwise inaccessible, he is haunted by unsettled perplexities, doubts, anxieties, thoughts.

This attitude of mind must have been very common in Christ's own time, many persons must have shrunk from the responsibility of determining for themselves what they ought to think of Him. Many now do the same. They wish to overlook Him and pass on into life as if He were not in their path. But how foolish if He be the one foundation on whom a life can safely be built. Men do not think of sin as a permanent foundation—they only think of it as a temporary expedient—practises get into a man's life which he does not like to think of as permanent, but only as serving present turns. They do not deliberately choose anything as permanently satisfactory, cannot bring their minds to the idea of being built *in* and settled finally, even though they have some consciousness that it were wise to be so. Those who thus overlook Christ and try to pass on into life as if He were not, damage their own character, because they know He is there, and until they make up their minds about Him, life is a mere make-believe. It is thus they are bruised on this stone of stumbling. They are practising upon themselves, and are not true to their own convictions. They do not walk steadily and uprightly as those whose path is ascertained and assured, but they stumble as those who are still tripped up and held back by something they have not taken account of. Just as a person who feels he has forgotten something, cannot give his mind fully to what is before him, but is held back by the unconscious effort to remember, so here the spirit that has yet to take account of Christ and decide regarding Him is held back and distracted. Besides, this unwillingness to face facts fairly, this desire to do for a time without Christ, and as if He were not in our path, is apt to produce a habitual falseness in the spirit. You may be unconscious of any such process, but many processes go on in us quite as effectually without as with our intention. Those which are fatal to the body do so. Each refusal to determine regarding Christ makes your conscience blunter, your heart less open to righteous and reasonable influence. It may be by a very little, yet it does. The frost of a minute, or of thirty minutes, may be imperceptible in its result, or it may only draw a few pretty lines upon the water, but it is frost all the same, and is gradually forming a strength of surface which no hammer can break, nor any fire melt. By trying, then, to get past Christ and make a life for yourself without Him, by trying to build on some other foundation, you are both trying to do what everything is arranged to defeat, and you are injuring your own character, not yielding to the influences that you feel to be good, nor listening to convictions which you shrewdly suspect to be reasonable.

This bruised condition, however, is remediable. The second action of the stone on the builder is described as final. The stone, which is of sufficient massiveness to uphold a world, falls upon the unhappy opposer, and the living, hopeful man lies an undistinguishable mass. At once slain and buried, those who determinedly opposed Christ lie oppressed by that which might have been their joy. Their dwelling and refuge becomes their tomb. Every excellence of Christ they have leagued against themselves. It is their everlasting shame that they were ashamed of Him. The faithfulness, truth, and love of Christ, that is to say, the qualities whose existence is all that any saved man ever had to depend upon, the qualities in the knowledge and faith of which the weakest and most heartless sinner sets out boldly and hopefully to eternity, these all now torment with crushing remorse those who have despised them. Do not suppose this is an extravagant figure used by our Lord to awe His enemies, and that no man will ever suffer a doom which can be fairly represented in these terms. It is a statement of fact. Things are to move on eternally in fulfilment of the will of Christ. He is identified with all that is righteous, all that is wise, all that is ultimately successful. To oppose His course, to endeavour to defeat His object, to attempt to work out an eternal success apart from Him is as idle as to seek to stop the earth in its course, or to stand in the path of a stone avalanche in order to stem it. His kingdom is an everlasting kingdom— He has become the Head of our race, that in Him we may together be led on to everlasting prosperity and righteousness.

The whole forward movement of individuals and of the race must be made on the lines laid down by Christ, and the time is coming when this shall be so plainly manifested that all who have not His spirit shall feel that all power has left them, and shall see the whole stream of life and progress flow past them, leaving them stranded and wrecked and useless. For a long time it may be doubtful in a country and in national affairs whether progress and prosperity are bound up with one party or another, with one spirit in trade and in government or with another, and men take their sides and adopt their several causes according to their tastes and judgment; but a day comes when the one party is put to confusion, and when it is entirely left behind by the current of events. So is it here, but in a far more momentous sense. It is not only national affairs that are governed and guided by certain deep laws that the craftiest statesman has no power whatever to alter; but the affairs of the individual, of each one of us, and of all men together, similarly move onwards according to certain immutable moral laws. These are revealed to us in Christ, that we may know and appropriate them. For, just in proportion as we do so, and attach ourselves to Him, and feel the power and beauty of His way and of His spirit, shall we ourselves stand with Him when all opposition has slunk away ashamed, and enter with Him on the great future which will open to those who are capable of taking a part in it. What, then, you feel it in you to do by God's grace in the way of bending your will to what is right, of subduing the evil in you which you see can but lead to death and disturbance, these things do, hoping in Him who has promised to return and reign eternally.

XI.
THE MARRIAGE OF THE KING'S SON.

"*And when the chief priests and Pharisees had heard his parables, they perceived that he spake of them. But when they sought to lay hands on him, they feared the multitude, because they took him for a prophet. And Jesus answered and spake unto them again by parables, and said, The kingdom of heaven is like unto a certain king, which made a marriage for his son, and sent forth his servants to call them that were bidden to the wedding: and they would not come. Again, he sent forth other servants, saying, Tell them which are bidden, Behold, I have prepared my dinner: my oxen and my fatlings are killed, and all things are ready: come unto the marriage. But they made light of it, and went their ways, one to his farm, another to his merchandise: and the remnant took his servants, and entreated them spitefully, and slew them. But when the king heard thereof, he was wroth: and he sent forth his armies, and destroyed those murderers, and burned up their city. Then saith he to his servants, The wedding is ready, but they which were bidden were not worthy. Go ye therefore into the highways, and as many as ye shall find, bid to the marriage. So those servants went out into the highways, and gathered together all as many as they found, both bad and good: and the wedding was furnished with guests. And when the king came in to see the guests, he saw there a man which had not on a wedding garment: and he saith unto him, Friend, how camest thou in hither not having a wedding garment? And he was speechless. Then said the king to the servants, Bind him hand and foot, and take him away, and cast him into outer darkness; there shall be weeping and gnashing of teeth. For many are called, but few are chosen."*
—MATT. xxi. 45—xxii. 14.

THE MARRIAGE OF THE KING'S SON.

MATT. xxi. 45—xxii. 14.

THIS parable is spoken to the same mixed crowd as the parable of the Two Sons and the parable of the Wicked Husbandmen. Sorely hit by the two former parables, the chief priests and Pharisees would fain have put a stop to this kind of teaching, but they feared the people. Public opinion here, as often elsewhere, was healthier than the opinion of the clique which had the official guidance of ecclesiastical and theological affairs. Public opinion was too markedly in favour of Jesus just at this time for the Pharisees to ignore or brave it. They felt they must take it into account, and either wait for a turn in the tide, or compass their end by craft, and secretly. While they hesitate and stand measuring the heartiness of the crowd in Jesus' favour, and considering how far they may venture, this third parable is launched against them.

The object of it is still the same—to set in a vivid light the guilt of the Jewish leaders in rejecting Christ, and the punishment which in consequence was to fall upon them; but to this third parable an appendix is added, which is even more striking than the parable itself—an appendix spoken, as we shall see, rather for the sake of the crowd than as a warning to the Pharisees.

Already in His parables our Lord had compared the kingdom of God to a feast, for the sake of illustrating the rude, discourteous, and mistaken way in which men deal with God's invitations. There are occasions on which men combine to be happy, meet for the understood purpose of enjoyment, so that anything which interrupts or represses the hilarity of the company is frowned upon as out of place and inopportune. Matters of great importance are postponed, questions requiring much gravity in their discussion are avoided, anything that might irritate or slightly annoy or discompose any single guest is excluded, and, in short, everything is arranged to admit of free, unrestrained mirth. And when such occasions are public, he who refuses to join in the national festivity is looked upon as a traitor, and he who has private griefs is expected to keep them in abeyance, "to anoint his head and wash his face that he appear not unto men to fast." Disloyalty could scarcely assume a more marked form than if a man being invited to share the festal joy of his king on some such worthy occasion as that here adduced, were either to refuse the invitation, or, accepting it, were to conduct himself with so sullen and rude a demeanour as to show that his feelings were quite out of harmony with his host's. Such a man would be at once recognised as disaffected and a rebel, and also as a rebel who had chosen a singularly unfortunate and discourteous mode of exhibiting his rebellion.

But the speciality of this parable is that the feast to which the king invites His subjects is a marriage feast. Prominence is given to the circumstance that the host is a king, and that the occasion of the feast is the marriage of His Son.

It is obvious how this figure was suggested to the mind of Christ. Long before His time the relation between husband and wife had been used to exhibit the devotedness and fidelity with which God gives Himself to men, as well as the intimacy and loving care to which He admits them. And the close alliance between God and men which was thus expressed, was actually consummated in the person of Jesus Christ. His assumption of humanity into perfect union with His own Divine nature was the actual marriage of God and man. In Him God and man are made one—so truly and perfectly one, that whereas formerly marriage was used to illustrate this union, now this union stands as the ideal to which marriage may aspire, but which it can never reach. It is a union which has the characteristics of marriage. It is the result of love and choice, not of nature; and it implies that the stronger party assume the responsibilities and watch over the interests of the weaker. The marriage is formed that the stronger party may have fuller opportunity to help and serve the weaker. God then might reasonably expect that men should, at least on this occasion, recognise that God and they constituted one kingdom and cause. Well might He expect that now, at least, they should rejoice with Him. It is their nature that is seated on the throne, their rights that are thus secured, their prosperity that is thus guaranteed. And yet, though proclamation had been made of the coming festivities, though due invitation had been given, and though, finally, John had been sent to say that now all things were ready and to herald the bridegroom in visible form through their streets, the people had listened with dead indifference, as if it had been a kingdom in the moon that was spoken of, and as if God had wholly mistaken in supposing that such an event had any bearing at all on them or their interests.

This union of God and man that is as natural as love, and as supernatural as God—this union, consummated in Christ, is the foundation of our hope. Apart from this we may find some little help in the hour of temptation, some faint glimmering of hope in the time of trouble, but nothing that can quite satisfy and bring to us a perfect light—nothing that can give us God, the Highest of all, the Eternal, the Almighty, the unfailing Love and Life. Jesus Christ blesses mankind not by His superior moral teaching mainly, nor only by His giving us a clearer knowledge of God than other teachers have done, but by His bringing God into human life, by showing us our God suffering with and for us, by bringing God to work among us and in our place, and thus to lift humanity, by a power Divine, to its highest level. It is by bringing thus a new thing into the world, the fulness of God into human life, that He has done that which no one but He could do, and which merits the gratitude of every man. He has thus become the true Bridegroom of men, the joy and help of us all. That was a memorable expression of Napoleon's when he said, "Jesus Christ has succeeded in making of every human soul an appendage to His own." He has made Himself the indispensable person to us all—the indispensable "fellow-worker with each man in the realisation of his supreme destiny."

The earnest sincerity of God in seeking our good in this matter is illustrated in the parable by one or two unmistakable traits—first, by the king's willing observance of every form of courtesy. Among ourselves there are certain forms, an etiquette, which a host who is anxious to please his guests is careful to conform to. There are ways of putting an invitation which make it almost impossible even for the reluctant to withhold acceptance. In the East one of these forms is the sending of a second messenger to announce the actual readiness of the feast. In countries where no memoranda are written, and where no fixed hours are observed or appointed, such a final and second invitation is almost necessary; or, if not necessary, does at least pleasantly display the cordiality of the host. To this form God condescended. He not only sent invitations by the prophets, bidding the Jews expect this festivity, but when it was ready He sent John to remind them and to bring them. So it is always. Because God is so true in his purpose to bless you, therefore is He most careful of all your feelings, picking each smallest stone out of your path that might cause you to stumble and take offence, leaving the reluctant without apology. God does not invite you to what has no existence, nor to what is not worth going so far to get, nor on terms it is impossible to fulfil, nor in such a manner that no man who respects himself can accept it. On the contrary, what God offers you is that in which He Himself rejoices. He offers you fellowship with His own Son, He offers you righteousness and love, and He offers this to you with the observance of every form that could prove consideration of your feelings, and in a way which involves that every one who really wishes to be blessed will receive all the help he requires in striving to be so.

2. Another proof of the earnestness of God in His invitation is His wrath against the murderers who had refused it. You are not much offended at one who refuses an invitation you have given in jest, or for form's sake, half hoping it would not be accepted. God is angry because you have treated in jest and made light of what has been most earnest to Him; because you have crossed Him in the sincerest purpose to bless you; because after He has at the greatest expense, not only of wealth and exertion, but of life, provided what He knows you need, you act towards Him as if He had done nothing that deserves the least consideration. This acceptance or rejection of God's offers that we come and talk over, often as if the whole matter were in our hands and we might deal with it as we arrange for a journey or an evening's amusement, is to God the most earnest matter. If God is in earnest about anything, it is about this; if the whole force of His nature concentrates on any one matter it is on this; if anywhere the amplitude and intensity of Divine earnestness, to which the most impassioned

human earnestness is as the idle vacant sighing of the summer air, if these are anywhere in action, it is in the tenderness and sincerity with which He invites you to Himself. There may be nothing so trivial as to be powerless to turn you from God's message, but nothing is so important as to turn Him from seeing how you receive it. You may think His invitation the least interesting of all subjects, you may in point of fact scarcely ever seriously consider whether it is to be accepted or not, whether it is an invitation, whether you might act upon it, and why you do not—the whole matter of God's offer to you may be unreal, but your answer is matter of God's consideration, and nothing can so occupy Him as to turn His observation from you. No glad tidings from any other part of His government can so fill His ear as to drown your sullen refusal of His grace. To save sinners from destruction is His grand purpose, and success in other parts of His government does not repay Him for failure here. And to make light of such an earnestness as this, an earnestness so wise, so called for, so loving, pure, and long-suffering, so Divine, is terrible indeed. To *have been* the object of such earnest love, to have had all the Divine attributes and resources set in motion to secure my eternal bliss, and to know myself capable of making light (making light!) of such earnestness as this, this surely is to be in the most forlorn and abject condition that any creature can reach.

The last scene in this parable comes upon us unexpectedly, and forms indeed an appendix introducing a new lesson, and directed to a special section in the audience. No doubt our Lord perceived that parables such as He had been uttering were open to misconstruction. Ill-living and godless persons, coarse, covetous, and malicious men might be led to fancy that it mattered very little how they had lived, or what they were. They saw that the gates of the kingdom were thrown open, that all indiscriminately were invited to enter, that God made no distinctions, saying to one, "I cannot forget your former neglect," to another, "I do not wish your presence," to a third, "You are too far gone in sin, I do not invite you." It had been made quite clear to them by these parables that they themselves were as free to enter the kingdom as those religious men they had been accustomed to consider so much more in God's favour than they were. This perception of the absolute unconditioned freedom of entrance, this sense borne in upon their mind that they were the objects of God's love and invitation, might possibly lead them to overlook the great moral change requisite in all who enter God's presence and propose to hold intercourse with Him. It is to disabuse them of the idea that the acceptance of God's invitation entails no alteration in their habits and spirit, that this appendix is added.

This object is gained by setting before them an instance in which one who accepted the invitation was convicted of a contempt of the host even greater than that which was involved in rejecting his invitation. He entered the banquetting hall without a wedding garment, appeared at the King's table in just the dress in which he had been found in the streets by the servants. But had he any means of obtaining a dress more in keeping with the occasion? Was he not perhaps a man so poor that he could afford no preparation of any kind? Had this been so, it would have been pleaded in excuse. But no doubt the parable supposes that the not unusual custom of providing for the guests the needed garment had been adopted; a provision which this guest had despised and refused; he had pushed past the officious servants who would have clothed him. It is this that constituted the man's audacity and guilt. Similar audacity in entering the king's presence without putting on the robe sent by the king for that purpose, has been known to cost a prime minister his life. A traveller who was invited, with the ambassadors he accompanied, to the table of the Persian king, says:—
" We were told by the officer that we, according

to their usage, must hang the splendid vests that were sent us from the king over our dresses, and so appear in his presence. The ambassadors at first refused, but the officer urged it so earnestly, alleging, as also did others, that the omission would greatly displease the king, since all other envoys observed such a custom, that at last they consented, and hanged, as did we also, the splendid vests over their shoulders." So at this marriage, dresses had been provided by the king. The guests who had been picked off the streets were not told to go home and do the best they could for their dress, but in the palace, in the vestibule of the banquet-hall each man was arrayed in the dress the king wished to see worn.—Possibly this man who declined the offered garment had a dress of his own he grudged to cover. Possibly he thought he was as well dressed as need be. He would stroll in superciliously as a patron or spectator, thinking it very fit for those poor, coarse-clothed and dirty people to make use of the king's wardrobe, but conscious of no speck nor uncleanliness in his own raiment that should cause him to make any alteration of it.

Neither is this a formal and artificial custom representing a formal and artificial method of judging men. In point of fact this rejection of the marriage-dress is proof of alienation of spirit, disaffection, want of sympathy with the feelings of the king. The man who could refuse the festive dress on such an occasion must lack the festive spirit, and is therefore a "spot in the feast." It is a real and internal, not a merely formal and external distinction that exists between him and the rest of the guests. He sits there out of harmony with the spirit of the occasion, despising the exultation and mirth of his neighbours, and disloyal to his king. Therefore is his punishment swift and severe. The eye of the king that travels round the tables and carries welcome and hearty recognition, gladdening all his loyal subjects, is suddenly arrested upon this unseemly, audacious, unjustifiable intruder. As every guest turns to see the cause of the changed expression in the face that lights up the whole feast, there with head that would, but cannot, hang, with horror-stricken eye rivetted upon the face of the king, stands the despiser of the wedding-garment—speechless—all his guilt and easy confidence gone, fearful misgivings sliding into his heart, quailing and fainting beneath that just and pitiful eye that empties him of all self-deceit, of all self-confidence, of all untruth. He welcomes the attendants who hurry him from the gaze of the assembled guests and the brilliant lights of the hall; but not the outer darkness of an Eastern street, not the pitchy blackness in which he lies unseen and helpless, can hide him from that gaze of His Lord which he feels to be imprinted on his conscience for evermore. It is that which pursues him, that which makes him outcast from all consolation and all hope, that he has alienated his Lord, has been branded by his king, has forfeited the approval and favour of Him whose recognition and fellowship carry with them all joy, and hope, and blessing.

Does this man's conduct signify anything to ourselves? Does his doom cover any great truth that concerns ourselves? How idle it seems to ask the question. Is there any commoner way of dealing with God's invitation than that which this man adopted? He had no deep love for his king, no grateful and humbling sense of his kindness, no perception of what was due to him, but with the blundering stupidity of godlessness, thought selfishness would carry him through, and ran right upon his doom. What is commoner than this self-complacency, this utter blindness to the fact that God is holy, and that holiness must therefore be the rule everywhere; what is commoner than the feeling that we are well enough, that we shall somehow pass muster, that as we mean to take our places among the heavenly guests we shall surely not be ejected? How hard it is for any of us fully to grasp the radical nature of the inward change that is required if we are to be meet for the inheritance of the saints in light. Conformity to God, ability to rejoice with God and in God, humble and devoted reverence, a real willingness to do honour to the King's Son, these are great attainments; but these constitute our wedding-garment, without which we cannot remain in His presence nor abide His searching gaze. It will come to be a matter between each one of you singly and Him, and it is the heart you bear towards Him that will determine your destiny. No mere appearance of accepting His invitation, no associating of yourself with those who love Him, no outward entrance into His presence, no making use of the right language is anything to the purpose. What is wanted is a profound sympathy with God, a real delight in what is holy, a radical acceptance of His will,—in other words, and as the most untutored conscience might see, what is wanted is a state of mind in you which God can delight in, and approve of, and hold fellowship with. To His table, to His everlasting company, to Himself and His love He invites you, and in order to accept this, the only, invitation He gives (for there are no degrees, no outer and inner circles, no servants made of those who will not be friends)—in order to accept this invitation, or in the acceptance of it, acceptance of God, of His spirit, character, and ways is necessary. There is no real acceptance of the invitation, no abiding entrance into God's favour where there is no growing likeness to God; without this it is mere word and self-deception. "Know ye not that the unjust shall not inherit the kingdom of God? Be not deceived: neither fornicators, nor idolaters, nor adulterers, nor effeminate, nor thieves, nor covetous, nor drunkards, nor revilers, nor extortioners shall inherit the kingdom of God."

For "many are called, but few chosen." To all of us the invitation comes: there is no man whom God does not desire to see enjoying His bounty. There is no question about the invitation—you have it—good and bad alike are invited, and yet even among those who seem to accept it, there is sometimes lacking that which can alone give them a permanent place in His presence and favour. There is no real sympathy with God, no pleasure in those matters which He deems important, no similarity of spirit—in a word, no real goodness. This is a state of spirit which will one day develope into a *consciousness* that we have nothing in common with God.

But, in conclusion, there is abundant encouragement in this parable to all who are willing and desirous to put on the Lord Jesus. As the poor people picked up by the servants of the king would have felt very awkward about their dress, and could not in decency have accepted the invitation had they not been assured that a suitable dress would be given them; so should we feel very awkward indeed, if, when summoned into God's presence, there should remain in us anything to make us feel out of place, uneasy, fearful. But the invitation itself guarantees the provision of all that follows it. It is the first business of every host to make his guest feel at home, and therefore does God provide us not only with great outward blessings, but with all that can make us feel easy and glad in His presence. Fellowship with Him is indeed reverential, for He is our King: but being our Father there will be in it also more of the exuberant delight of a family gathering than of the stiffness of a formal state banquet throughout which we long for the termination, or are hindered from all enjoyment through fear of doing something out of place.

Though, therefore, there are many called but few chosen, there is no reason why you should not be among the few. For God not only offers enjoyment, but also power to enjoy. If you could not be easy in God's presence without great alterations in your character, these alterations will be made. The *bona fide* invitation is your guarantee that they will be made. If you could not be easy in God's presence without knowing that He was fully aware of all you had thought and done against Him, and forgave it you; if you could not eat at the table of one against whom you harboured ill-will; if you could not enjoy anything in company thoroughly uncongenial, whose conversation was all of subjects quite uninteresting to you; if you are conscious that in order to enjoy any entertainment the prime requisite is that you have a genuine admiration and love for the host—then this will all be communicated to you on your acceptance of God's invitation. Do you always feel that God's holiness is too high and distant for fellowship? But consider how Christ drew men and women to Him. No one ever created such a passion of devoted love as He. Consider Him and you will at length learn to think more wisely of holiness. Are you conscious that your habitual leanings and likings are earthly, that as yet you are more at home in other companies than in God's? Does your unfitness even more than your unworthiness deter you—does your want of ability to find your joy in God alarm you more than your guilt? Still you see here that God invites you as you are, and those whom He casts out are only those who have so fond a confidence in themselves as to think they are fit enough for His presence as they stand.

XII.
THE TEN VIRGINS.

"Then shall the kingdom of heaven be likened unto ten virgins, which took their lamps, and went forth to meet the bridegroom. And five of them were wise, and five were foolish. They that were foolish took their lamps, and took no oil with them: but the wise took oil in their vessels with their lamps. While the bridegroom tarried, they <u>all</u> slumbered and slept. And at midnight there was a cry made, Behold, the bridegroom cometh; go ye out to meet him. Then all those virgins arose, and <u>trimmed their lamps</u>. And the foolish said unto the wise, Give us of your oil; for our lamps are gone out. But the wise answered, saying, <u>Not so</u>; lest there be not enough for us and you: but go ye rather to them that sell, and buy for yourselves. And while they went to buy, the bridegroom came; and <u>they that were ready went in with him to the marriage: and the door was shut</u>. Afterwards came also the other virgins, saying, Lord, Lord, open to us. But he answered and said, Verily I say unto you, I know you not. Watch therefore, for ye know neither the day nor the hour wherein the Son of man cometh."—MATT. xxv. 1-13.

THE TEN VIRGINS.

MATT. xxv. 1-13.

THE prolonged discourse of which this parable forms a striking part was uttered in reply to a very natural question which the disciples had put to our Lord. In ignorance of what was chiefly engaging His thoughts, and in simple-minded, rustic admiration of the metropolis, they had been taking Him round to show Him the marvels of the now completed temple. And well might they expect to hear their own exclamations of surprise and overwhelming admiration echoed from every one who in their day "walked about Zion" and marked her bulwarks, or gazed on the astounding pile of marble that crowned the opposite summit of Moriah. Buildings of similar magnificence were scarcely elsewhere to be seen. It can scarcely have been with cold contempt for those stupendous architectural works, but rather with deep sorrow and compassion that our Lord, after silently gazing upon them, or entering with sympathy into the enthusiasm of his companions at last let fall the unexpected word,

"Verily I say unto you there shall not be left here one stone upon another, that shall not be thrown down." It was inevitable that the disciples should eagerly desire to know when this catastrophe was to occur. "Tell us when shall these things be, and what shall be the sign of Thy coming and of the end of the world."

Our Lord's reply to this question is, that the day and the hour of His coming are known to the Father only, and that therefore the only way to be prepared for that hour is to be always ready, prepared for any hour and every hour. This is the lesson which He means the parable to convey, and which He expressly draws in the words, "Watch, therefore, for ye know neither the day nor the hour when the Son of man cometh." And we must beware of pressing this or any parable to say more than it was meant to say. We get what it was intended to give when by its vivid imagery we are practically aroused to the necessity of being always prepared for our Lord's coming. We may therefore dismiss a great deal of minute allegorizing and searching for hidden meanings in little turns of expression and parabolic accessories with the words of one of the Reformers who says, "It is nothing at all to the purpose to speculate and refine about virginity and lamps and oil and those who sell oil. These refined speculations are the trifles of allegorizers. But the one idea that is of moment is, that they who are really prepared shall enter into the joy of the Lord, while the unprepared shall be excluded." Or we may say with Calvin himself:—"Some expositors torment themselves greatly in explaining the *lamps*, and the *vessels*, and the *oil;* but the simple and genuine meaning of the whole is just this, that it is not enough to have a lively zeal for a while. We must have in addition a perseverance that never tires."

Neither need we spend time on the customs from which the parable draws its imagery. Let it suffice to read the words of one of the most accurate describers of what is to be seen in India. "At a marriage," he says, "the procession of which I saw some years ago, the bridegroom came from a distance, and the bride lived at Serampore, to which place the bridegroom was to come by water. After waiting two or three hours, at length, near midnight, it was announced, as if in the very words of Scripture, 'Behold the bridegroom cometh, go ye out to meet him.' All the persons employed now lighted their lamps, and ran with them in their hands to fill up their stations in the procession. Some of them had lost their lights, and were unprepared; but it was then too late to seek them, and the cavalcade moved forward to the house of the bride, at which place the company entered a large and splendidly illuminated area before the house covered with an awning, where a great multitude of friends, dressed in their best apparel, were seated upon mats. The bridegroom was carried in the arms of a friend, and placed upon a superb seat in the midst of the company, where he sat a short time, and then went into the house, the door of which was immediately shut, and guarded by sepoys. I and others expostulated with the doorkeepers, but in vain. Never was I so struck with our Lord's beautiful parable as at this moment: *and the door was shut.*"

This imagery so familiar to our Lord's hearers was used on this occasion to illustrate chiefly these three things: the meaning of our Lord's command to watch; its reason; and the means of fulfilling it. It illustrates the *meaning* of the command; shewing us that it does not mean, "Be ye always on the watch," but "Be always prepared." The fisherman's wife who spends her time on the pier-head watching for the boats, cannot be so well prepared to give her husband a comfortable reception as the woman who is busy about her household work, and only now and again turns a longing look seaward. None of the virgins were on the watch for the bridegroom, but some of them were nevertheless prepared for His coming. It is impossible for us to be always looking out for the coming of Christ, but it is quite possible to be prepared for His coming. Our life is to bear evidence that one of the things we take into account is the approach of our Lord.

2. It illustrates also the *reason* of the command. No one can tell when this second great interruption of the world's even course is to take place. It may be nearer than some expect; or as the parable shows, it may be more distant than some expect. The expectation of a speedy termination of things which so largely prevailed in the first Christian generation might have been moderated by the wide circulation of this parable. The virgins who neglected to carry reserve-flasks of oil were those who expected the bridegroom would soon appear. They did not anticipate a long delay; they made no provision for continuance. Had the hour been a fixed one they would have been prepared, but they were betrayed by its uncertainty. And no doubt if any one could say with authority, "The Lord is to come on Tuesday first," a very large number of persons would at once prepare as best they could to meet Him. If the belief really grew up within them that on a certain day not far distant they must face their Lord, that belief would certainly produce a multitude of thoughts and some efforts at preparation. It is, then, after all, your baseless supposition that the Lord will not come quickly that betrays

you into carelessness. This parable assures you you have no ground for saying, "My Lord delayeth His coming." You really do not know how near He is.

And if any one feels, "Well, this then comes to no more than an appeal to fear. The appeal made by the parable is grounded on the assumption that Christians will be better men, and do more if they expect to be quickly summoned into Christ's presence,"—if this be felt, it can only be said in reply that fear is in many circumstances the equivalent of prudence, and a very wholesome motive; and further, that the expectation of Christ's coming does not give rise only to fear, but also to hope; that it braces the Christian's energies, and in accordance with human nature quickens the spiritual life. Or if any one feels that to have stimulated all past generations with the expectation of an event which did not after all occur, is artificial and unworthy, it should be enough to reflect that the beneficial system of insurance proceeds on principles to a large extent similar.

3. The parable shews us *how* we are to prepare for meeting the Lord. We are to be prepared to join in the festal celebration of His coming. We are to be in a position to join with those who add lustre to His presence, who give Him a hearty welcome, and who enter with Him into His joy. We are prepared for His

coming if we are in the spirit of the occasion, and if we are furnished with what may fit us for suitably appearing in His company. The lamps of the virgins were meant to lend brilliancy to the scene; they were intended as a festal illumination. The virgins whose lamps burned brightly were not ashamed to be seen forming part of the bridal company. They were in keeping with it. Conscience will tell us what numbers us among the wise or among the foolish. Everything in us that heartily welcomes Christ's presence, and heartily rises to do Him honour; everything about us that can reflect any brightness or glory on Him; everything that makes us better than blots and blacknesses in His retinue; everything that will seem a suitable accompaniment in the triumph of a holy Redeemer, is a preparation for Christ's coming.

The parable is not addressed to those who have never made any preparation for Christ's coming, but to those who have not made sufficient preparation. It reminds us that all who may at one time show similar preparedness for Christ's presence do not in the end show the same. Of those who start with similar intentions and similar external appearance a number fail to fulfil their original intention, and in the end belie their promising appearance. It is the same everywhere: in severe marches, prolonged and fatiguing enterprises and labours, a number always tail off and are not forthcoming at the final muster. The number who at any period of their life really go forth to meet their Lord, delighting to do Him honour and seeking His presence, may not be very large; but it is much larger than the number who maintain their preparedness to the end. The reason of this so frequent failure is here declared. The folly of the foolish virgins consisted in this, that while the wise took oil, they took none: that is to say, made no provision against any delay in the time of the Bridegroom's appearance. They lit their lamps, but made no provision for feeding them: the flame was to all appearance satisfactory, but the source of it was defective. And without running the figure too hard, we may say that those who in the end of their life fail to show as much fitness for Christ's presence as they did at some previous period, fail because they have been all along superficial and have never been filled with grace at the source, have not had the root of the matter in them.

The foolish virgins, then, are a warning to all who are tempted to make conversion everything, edification nothing; who cultivate religion for a season and then think they have done enough; who were religious once, can remember the time when they had very serious thoughts, and very solemn resolutions, but who have made no earnest effort, and are making none, to maintain within themselves the life they once began. The wise are those who recognise that they must have within them that which shall enable them to endure to the end —not only impressions, right impulses, tender feelings, but ineradicable beliefs and principles which will at all times produce all right impulse and feeling. It is not in vain that our nature is made as it is made. In body and soul things are so ordered that one part aids and feeds another part. Without a good digestion no other function can be thoroughly well performed; as well performed as it might be. And in our spiritual nature, our feelings and impulses are nourished by our beliefs and perceptions. If we recognise the truth, if we have come to an assured and settled conviction that Christ has lived, and that He now lives, if our perceptions and beliefs are bringing us in contact with the truth, with Christ, and with things unseen, then we may expect to continue to the end.

Another point may be accepted from this part of the Parable: that there must be regard paid both to the outward and inward life. The vessel of oil is not enough without the burning lamp; nor the lamp merely lighted and with no supply of oil. There is a something which makes you worthy of entering with Christ into lasting joy. And this something is not an exhibition of the external marks of a Christian, neither is it the certainty that once you had inward grace; but it is the continuous maintenance, to the end, both of the outward works which manifest, and of the inward graces which are the life of a Christian. The inward life of the soul and the outward expression of that life bear to one another an essential relation. On the one hand, if you do not constantly renew your supply of grace, if you do not carefully see to the condition of your own spirit, your good works will soon become less frequent, less sincere, and less lovely: your flame will burn low. But, on the other hand, if you tend only the life of your own soul, if you seek only to possess as much grace as possible for yourself, if you ask for the Holy Spirit and yet do none of those things in which the Spirit would naturally express Himself, if you do not let your light shine before and upon men in the actual circumstances you are placed in, then you will soon find that your internal life begins to stagnate and corrupt.

To a healthy Christian life these two things are essential. A vessel of oil is, in itself, of no use on a dark night. The oil is not light, and might as well be water unless a light be added. And a burning wick which lasts only for half a minute, is only disappointing and tantalising. A Christian must not only feel right but do right; and must not only do right but feel right. To be filled with the Spirit you have but to pray. You cannot manufacture nor create that which can sustain your spiritual life : God only can give it, and give it He does, gladly and liberally, in answer to your requests. And having the Spirit you must use Him; letting your light shine not so as to show yourself more conspicuously, but so as to help on others in their dark and doubtful way through this life ; by dealing fairly with them, by being generous and considerate, by doing the best you can for every one you have to do with in any capacity.

This is the reason why many of us feel slightly jarred in spirit when we hear converts rising in a confession-meeting one after another and saying, "I was saved last Wednesday night," "I was saved on the 18th February," "I was saved on the 12th March," and so on. It is not that we do not believe that they are speaking the truth, but that we know that they have yet to be tested by life. We rejoice with them because they have found their Saviour ; we tremble for them because we know that they have yet to work out their own salvation through years of temptation. All that their confession means is, that their lamp is lit, but how long it will burn is quite another question.

They are merely in the condition of the ten virgins as they first went out, and only time can show whether they have oil or not. They may have been able to rejoice in Christ at a given hour last week or last month, and may at that hour have risen to greet Him, and there is nothing wrong in their declaring that such has been the case: but their trial has yet to take place; it has yet to be discovered whether, when many years have passed, they shall still be found rejoicing in Him. For in many cases it would appear as if conversion and salvation were looked upon as equivalents: in many cases there is a lack of soberminded counting of the cost, and a jubilation of spirit which would be more becoming at the close of the long fight of faith than at its commencement. You may say you are saved when you fairly put yourself into Christ's hand; but you must also remember that then your salvation is only beginning, and that you cannot, in the fullest sense, say you are saved until Christ has wrought in you a perfect conformity to Himself.

This being the distinction between the wise and foolish virgins, that which brings it to light is that the Bridegroom did not come while all the lamps were yet burning, and that during His delay they all slumbered and slept. This seems to mean no more than that all, having made such preparation as they judged sufficient "calmly and securely waited the approach of the Bridegroom." There can scarcely be any more than this meant by the sleep; nothing which would make the sleep culpable on the part of the wise, for we do not find that any evil consequence whatever followed to them; rather they would be all the fresher for their rest, the better prepared to enter on the joy. But the security which is excusable, and the repose which is necessary to one condition, is in another utter madness. Unconstrained mirth, eager pursuit of business, is one thing in the man who has just examined his books and made arrangements to meet all claims, but it is quite another thing in him who has made no such arrangements and does not know whether he can meet his engagements. So it is one thing to turn away your attention from the person and coming of Christ when you have made sure you are prepared to meet Him, and altogether another thing to turn your attention to other things in mere thoughtless security. It is one thing to engage in the business of this life, knowing that though your Lord find you in it, you have what will enable you to meet Him, the graces then required being really in you and ready to show themselves, though not at present called into exercise by the calculation, or the plan, or the work you are engaged in for the hour; but it is wholly another thing to plunge into the world's business without having once considered whether you have given sufficient attention to your preparedness for that event which may interrupt any day's business, or without keeping up a constant examination of the inward life of your spirit.

But we may learn from the slumber of the wise, as well as from the rash sleep of the foolish. There is a kind of sleep in which the sense of hearing, at least, is on the alert, and when by a skilful discrimination unattainable when awake, the sense takes note only of the one sound it waits for, so that the sound of a distant and watched-for footstep arouses to the keenest wakefulness. If you look on these weary, slumbering virgins, you see the lamps firmly grasped, and when you try to unclasp the slumbering but faithful fingers, every faculty is at once on the alert. Other noises do not awaken them, but before the cry, "The Bridegroom cometh" has ceased to echo in the porch that shelters them, they stand erect and are trimming their lamps. So should it be with us; whatever necessary occupation, whatever necessary saturation of our minds with the thoughts of this world's property, turns our direct attention from the approach of our Lord, there should still be an openness of sense in His direction, a settled persuasion that it is His voice that must be hearkened to, a predisposedness to attend rather to Him if He should call, an inwrought though latent expectation of His coming, a consciousness,' which but a whisper will arouse, that what we are here for is not to slumber, not to do what we might as well or better do anywhere else and with no hope of our Lord's coming, but still to meet Him. Through all the sleep of these virgins, dream would be chasing dream, they would be seeing bridal processions, gorgeous with all the gay and fantastic adornment which the closed eye so clearly sees, hearing sackbut and dulcimer and all kinds of music, and ever and anon starting to hear if the cry, "The Bridegroom cometh" were not real and summoning themselves. So through all the occupations of a Christian in which he is not watching for his Lord and trimming his lamp, there is, or should be, an under-current of expectation, ever keeping him in unconscious preparedness, occasionally roused into actual looking out to see. He is not always gazing forward, but ever and anon sends a messenger from the inmost citadel of his soul to enquire, "Watchman, what of the night?"

While they are thus all slumbering, and when their sleep is deepest, when the fatigue of watching is most felt, when things are stillest, and men count upon a few hours quiet and deliverance from care, "at midnight,' the cry is heard, "Behold, the Bridegroom cometh!" And now the difference between the really and apparently prepared is manifested. There is something terrible in the security of the foolish maintained up to the last. They, too, arise and trim their lamps; even though there is nothing but a quenched, foul wick, yet they seem to think still that matters are not so bad. They have but to ask oil of their pleasant companions. Not yet are they aware that their fate is already sealed. And this sudden and appalling reversal of their hopes, this mingling at a marriage feast of exultant joy and the most melancholy and calamitous ruin, seems intended to fix in our minds an idea opposite to, and that should extirpate the idle fancy that things somehow will come all right; that there is no real need of all this urgent warning and watching; that in a world governed by a good and loving God, and where things are going on now pretty tolerably and so very prosaically, there cannot occur those startling, unnatural, desolating events predicted in God's word. It seems so fearful and incredible a thing that a world men take so lightly and joyously should be quietly leading them on to eternal ruin, that men maintain their easy disposition to the last, and cannot believe that out of a life that may be jested or trifled away, consequences so lasting and so awful can possibly flow. Many things are needed to drive this security out of us, and many things are given us for this end. The virgins go out with no thought but of festivity, enjoyment, and happy excitement; five of them, before the night is gone, are found and left in the bitterest sorrow and self-reproach. "They that were ready went in to the marriage, and the door was shut."

In these words one seems to hear the decisive, final doom of the lost. The crash of the heavy dungeon door and the retiring footsteps are not more sickening to the heart of him that is left to die of hunger, than the heavy, sudden closing of this door that shuts in the saved and shuts out the lost. As the feeling of comfort inside the house increases when the storm howls around and shakes it, as if seeking an entrance that it cannot find, so does the misery of those left outside increase when they hear the sound of revelry and mirth, and see the warm lights thrown out on the darkness. They look round despairingly as the storm begins to rise, as the first moan of the gathering tempest nears and lights upon them, and warns them, as if in pity, of the blasts that follow as if in anger. But once the door is shut no piteous clamour outside can open it. No sense of the awful state of things outside, no willingness now to be within, avails to force it back upon its hinges. Every voice that wails for entrance is still met by the same chilling, hopeless reply, "I know you not." A new thing it is for that door to be shut. So long has it stood open, thrown wide back, that we forget there is a door that can shut that entrance; that it is not more useful now to let in, than one day to keep out. But the time comes when whosoever will shall not be saved; when it will be vain pointing men to the door; when whosoever is outside, there remains. And this time may be before you rise from where you now sit. No man can say it shall not. He who feels it most unfair to be hedged up thus to an hour, to be told it is unsafe and unreasonable to delay even so long, cannot assert that the end is further distant. To-day the door is open, to-morrow it may be too late to seek entrance. The hand that closes it may already be laid upon it.

It is foolishness, not wickedness, that is reprehended in these virgins—that is to say, in those who are represented by them. The wise man is he who shapes his conduct in accordance with the truth of things and with actual facts; the foolish man is he who shuts his eyes to what he does not wish to see, and fancies that somehow, though he can't tell how, things will go all right with him. He is, in fact, the ostrich who buries his head in the sand and fancies he has escaped because he has shut his eyes to what is hostile. The man who makes no preparation for the future is a foolish man. He may explain it to himself as he pleases, but to attempt an explanation is only to give further proof of his foolishness. He may see his way with perfect clearness a few paces before him, but if he does not see where it is to end, how can he tell whether he ought to go on even these few paces? The man who does not think, who does not consider whether he is prepared for the future or not, who does not seriously measure himself by every standard he can think of, and especially by the inevitable requirements of God and eternity, is a foolish man. He may be clever, brilliant in talk and very entertaining in company, he may be useful in business, he may be well-meaning, but he is foolish—has none of that wisdom which consists in seeing things as they actually are, and in conforming oneself to them. The man who at this present time is in point of fact leaving it to mere chance whether he is to be saved or lost, must surely feel that he is profoundly foolish.

Let us then meet Christ's intention in the parable, and see that for our part we are prepared for His coming. Let us make sure that the little flame once kindled is not already burning low. Let us be sure that we are living in constant communication with the source of all spiritual life; that the very spirit of Christ dwells in us richly. Is there one who feels that things are not with him as they ought to be, and that he has declined from the glad preparedness he once enjoyed, or even that he has never attained to a state in which any lustre could be thrown by him on the redeeming grace of Christ? To this person Christ speaks the parable. It is you He longs to see providing yourself with the material of everlasting goodness and everlasting joy. There is a Spirit offered you through whom you can become pure and loving, capable of good, at peace with yourself and with God. What response do you make to Christ's offers? Are you to turn away and let it be possible that the next summons you hear may be: "Behold the Bridegroom cometh, go ye out to meet Him?"

XIII.

THE TALENTS.

"*For the kingdom of heaven is as a man travelling into a far country, who called his own servants, and delivered unto them his goods. And unto one he gave five talents, to another two, and to another one; to every man according to his several ability; and straightway took his journey. Then he that had received the five talents went and traded with the same, and made them other five talents. And likewise he that had received two, he also gained other two. But he that had received one went and digged in the earth, and hid his lord's money. After a long time the lord of those servants cometh, and reckoneth with them. And so he that had received five talents came and brought other five talents, saying, Lord, thou deliveredst unto me five talents: behold, I have gained beside them five talents more. His lord said unto him, Well done, thou good and faithful servant: thou hast been faithful over a few things, I will make thee ruler over many things: enter thou into the joy of thy lord. He also that had received two talents came and said, Lord, thou deliveredst unto me two talents: behold, I have gained two other talents beside them. His lord said unto him, Well done, good and faithful servant; thou hast been faithful over a few things, I will make thee ruler over many things: enter thou into the joy of thy lord. Then he which had received the one talent came and said, Lord, I knew thee that thou art an hard man, reaping where thou hast not sown, and gathering where thou hast not strawed: and I was afraid, and went and hid thy talent in the earth: lo, there thou hast that is thine. His lord answered and said unto him, Thou wicked and slothful servant, thou knewest that I reap where I sowed not, and gather where I have not strawed: thou oughtest therefore to have put my money to the exchangers, and then at my coming I should have received mine own with usury. Take therefore the talent from him, and give it unto him which hath ten talents. For unto every one that hath shall be given, and he shall have abundance: but from him that hath not shall be taken away even that which he hath. And cast ye the unprofitable servant into outer darkness: there shall be weeping and gnashing of teeth.*"—MATT. xxv. 14-30.

THE TALENTS.

MATT. xxv. 14-30.

THIS parable illustrates the great principle which regulates the distribution of rewards and punishments in the kingdom of God—the principle that men shall be judged according to the means at their disposal. The "talents" represent everything over and above natural ability, by which men can advance the interests of the kingdom; position, opportunities, and especially the measure of grace given to each man. All the interests of Christ upon earth are entrusted to His people. He has distributed among us all that He values upon earth. Destroy from earth what men have and enjoy, and all that Christ prizes is gone. There is no interest of His carried forward without human labour; if His servants all cease to work, His cause on earth is at an end. And every servant of His is endowed with means enough to accomplish his own share in Christ's work. He may not have as much as others. But to be fair, there must be little put in the hands of the servant who can only make use of a little, and much put at the disposal of him who can manage a large amount. It is as easy—you may say—to make ten talents out of five, as to make four out of two; perhaps easier. Yes, if you choose the right man, but many a man who could make a small business pay, would ruin himself in a big one. Each gets what each can conveniently and effectively handle; and no one is expected to produce results which are quite out of proportion to his ability and his means.

And in order that the judgment may be fair, the reckoning is not made until "after a long time." We are not called upon to show fruit before autumn. The servants are not summoned to the reckoning while yet embarrassed by the novelty of their position; time is allowed them to consider, to calculate, to wait opportunities, to make experiments. The Lord does not quickly return in a captious spirit, but delays till the wise have had time to lay up great gains, and even the foolish to have learnt wisdom. So with ourselves: we cannot complain if strict account be taken at the end, because we really have time to learn how to serve our Lord. We have time to repair bad beginnings, to take thought, to make up in some degree for lost time. We are not hurried into mistakes and snatched to judgment, as if life were an ordeal we were passing through, where the slightest failure finishes our chances and is relentlessly watched for and insisted upon. We see well enough that with God it is quite otherwise; that He wishes us to succeed, will not observe our failures, winks at our shortcomings, and often repairs the ill we have done.

It is not without significance that the servant who did nothing at all for his master, was he who had received but one talent. No doubt those who have great ability are liable to temptations of their own; they may be more ambitious, and may find it difficult to serve their master with means which they see would bring in to themselves profits of a kind they covet. But such men are at all events not tempted to bury their talent. This is the peculiar temptation of the man who has little ability, and sullenly retires from a service in which he cannot shine and play a conspicuous part. His ambition outruns his ability, and while he envies the position of others, he neglects the duties of his own. Because he cannot do as much as he would, he will not do as much as he can. By showing no interest in that situation in life that God has seen fit he should fill, he would have us believe he is qualified for a higher.

There are many to whom this hint of the parable applies. You are in the same condemnation as this servant when you shrink from exercising your talent; because it is only one and a small one; when you refuse to do anything, because you cannot do a great deal; when you refuse to help, where you cannot lead; when you hesitate about aiding in some work, because those with whom you would be associated in it do it better, and show better in the doing of it than yourself; when you refuse to speak a word in behalf of Christ, because you could not satisfy your own taste, because you could not do it so well as some other person could; when you refuse to take some position, engage in some duty, be of some use in a certain department in which you would not excel, and would be recognised as surpassed by some others. This miserable fear of being mediocre, how many a good work has it prevented or crippled. If we wait till we are fully qualified to serve Christ, we shall never serve Him at all. If we cannot stoop to learn to do great things by doing very little things, we shall never do great things. The only known way to become a strong and full-grown man is to be first a little child.

It is a true proverb that "the sluggard is wiser in his own eyes than seven men that can render a reason." He can always justify his conduct. The insolence of this man's words is not intentional. He reads off correctly his own state of mind, and fancies that his conduct was appropriate and innocent. It was not his fault that his master was a man who struck terror into the hearts of his servants, and whom it was useless trying to please. And probably this man's account of the reason of his inactivity was accurate. All wrongness of conduct is at bottom based on a wrong view of God. Nothing so conduces to right action as right thoughts about God. If we think with this servant that God is hard, grudging to give and greedy to get, taking note of all shortcomings, but making no acknowledgment of sincere service, exacting the utmost farthing and making no abatement or allowance—if we one way or other virtually come to think that God never really delights in our efforts after good, and that whatever we attempt in our life He will coldly weigh and scorn, then manifestly we shall have no heart to labour for Him.

But this view of God is unpardonably narrow, and the action flowing from it is after all inconsistent. It is unpardonably wrong, and the very heartiness with which these other servants were greeted refutes it. You hear the hearty "well done" ringing through the whole palace—there is no hesitating scrutiny, no reminding them they had after all merely done what it was their duty to do—not at all—it is the genial, generous outburst of a man who likes to praise and hates to find people at fault; he has been hoping to get a good account of his servants, and it is far more joy in them than gratification in his increased property that prompts this exclamation of surprise and delight and approval. He feels himself much richer in the fidelity of his servants than in their gains. He has pleasure in promoting them, in bringing them up more nearly to his own rank and person, and in making them thus share in his own plans and arrangements and rule and joy.

Moreover, not only is the view of the master wrong, but the consequent action, as the master points out, is inconsistent. If the master is so slow to recognise sincere effort, so oppressive in his exactions, demanding bricks where he has given no straw, requiring impossible performances, and measuring all work by an impossible standard, is this a reason for making no effort to conciliate him? If you feared that, in the necessary hazard of business, you might lose your lord's talent, yet surely his anger would be as much aroused by inactivity as by unsuccessful efforts to serve him? Why did you not at least put his money into the hands of men who would have found a use for it, and would have paid you a good interest? If you were too timid to use the trust your lord left you, if you knew too little of business and the world's ways to venture on any self-devised investment, there were plenty of substantial, genuine undertakings into which you might have put your means. You could work under the guidance of some more masculine nature, who could direct and shelter you.

There are numberless ways in which the most slenderly equipped among us can fulfil the suggestion here given, and put our talent to the exchangers, into the hands of men who can use it. There is no lack of great works going on for our Lord to which we may safely attach ourselves, and in which our talent is rather used by the leaders of the work, invested for us, than left to our own discretion. Just as in the world there is such an endless variety of work needing to be done, that every one finds his niche, so there is no kind of ability that cannot be made use of in the kingdom of Christ. The parable does not acknowledge any servants who have absolutely nothing; some have little as compared with others, but all have some capacity to forward the interests of the absent master. Is every one of us practically recognizing this—that there is a part of the work he is expected to do? He may seem to himself to have only one talent that is not worth speaking about, but that one talent was given that it might be used, and if it be not used, there will be something lacking when reckoning is made which might and ought to have been forthcoming. Certainly there is something you can do, that is unquestionable; there is something that needs to be done which precisely you can do, something by doing which you will please Him whose pleasure in you will fill your nature with gladness. It *is* given to you to increase your Lord's goods.

But the law which is exhibited in this parabolic representation is also explicitly announced in the words: "For unto every one that hath shall be given, and he shall have abundance, but from him that hath not shall be taken away even that which he hath." This may be called the law of Spiritual Capital. It is a law with the operation of which we are familiar in nature, and in the commercial world. It is he who has even a little capital to begin with, and who makes a right use of it, who soon leaves far behind the man who has none, or who neglects to invest what he has. And the more this capital grows, the more rapidly and the more easily is it increased. After a certain point, it seems to increase by virtue of its own momentum. So in certain sicknesses, as soon as the crisis of the disease is past and a little health has been funded again in the patient's constitution, this rapidly grows to complete recovery. So with popularity, it begins one scarce knows how; but once begun, the tide flows apace. You may scarcely be able to say why one statesman or one author should be so immeasurably more popular than others; but

THE TALENTS.

so it is, that when once a beginning is made, tribute flows in naturally, as waters from all sides settle in a hollow. It is the same with the acquirement of knowledge: the difficulty is to get past a certain point, it is all uphill till then; but that point once gained, you reach the table lands and high levels of knowledge, where you begin to see all round you, and information that has been fragmentary, and therefore useless before, now pieces itself together and rapidly grows to complete attainment. Every thing you hear or see now seems by a law of nature to contribute to the fund you have already acquired. It claims kindred with it, and unites itself to it. "'Tis the taught already that profits by teaching."

It is this same law which regulates our attainment in the service of Christ. However little grace we seem to have to begin with, it is this we must invest, and so nurse it into size and strength. Each time we use the grace we have by responding to the demands made upon it, it <u>returns to us increased.</u> Our capital grows by an inevitable law. The efforts of young or inexperienced Christians to give utterance to the life that is in them may often be awkward, like the movements of most young animals. They may be able to begin only in a very small way, so small a way that sensitive persons are frequently ashamed to begin at all.

Having received Christ, they are conscious of new desires and of a new strength; they have a regard for Christ, and were they to assert this regard in the circumstances which call for its assertion, their regard would be deepened. They have a desire to serve Him, and were they to do so in those small matters with which they have daily concern, their desire and ability would be increased. Grace of any kind invested in the actual opportunities of life cannot come back to us as small as it was, but enlarged and strengthened.

Such grace then as we have, such knowledge as we have of what is due to others, to ourselves, and to God, let us give free expression to. Such investments of Christian principle as are within our reach let us make; such manifestations of a Christian temper and mind as our circumstances daily demand let us exhibit, and it must come to pass that we increase in grace. There is no other way whatever of becoming richly endowed in spirit than by trading with whatever we have to begin with. We cannot leap into a fortune in spiritual things; rich saints cannot bequeath us what their life-long toil has won; they cannot even lend us so that we may begin on borrowed capital. In the spiritual life all must be genuine; we must work our own way upwards, and by humbly and wisely laying out whatever we now possess, make it more or be for ever poor.

And yet how few avail themselves of this law, and lay up treasure in heaven. How few make great fortunes in the spiritual life. The mass of Christians never get even fairly started in a career which is at all likely to end in great saintliness of character and serviceableness. They act as if they had no capital of grace to begin with, no fund to trade upon; and they never make any more of it than they made the first week of their profession. They are not traders, every year increasing their stock and enlarging their gains, but they resemble men who receive a weekly wage, which is no more to-day than it was years ago. Is it not worthy of remark that after years of prayer and of concernment with the fountain of all spiritual life, there should be so small a fund of it laid up within ourselves? Is it not the fact that we seem to be living from hand to mouth, on the verge of bankruptcy, with no more between us and spiritual starvation than the day we believed? Are we conscious that our Christian principle has been deepening year by year? Can we count over our spiritual gains this day, and reckon up solid accumulations <u>of grace in our character?</u> Or are we still merely keeping the wolf from the door, and not always that? Are we making a bare shift to get through without absolutely breaking down? Is it all we can do to make ends meet, and to keep up in our own souls the idea that we are servants of Christ? Do we feel as if there were the thinnest partition between us and great sin? In a word, are we enriched with the "more abundance" of the well-doing servant, and do we find ourselves every way better equipped for all good work; or does even that which we once persuaded ourselves we had seem to be vanishing away?

But the parable reminds us that it is not only the careless who fail to use their talents to advantage, but that the same result sometimes follows from a deliberate but false conception of the service of Christ. As in the world, there are many who prefer comfort to wealth, and have no ambition to rank as millionaires, so in the Christian life many prefer what they conceive to be security to eminent saintliness. They do not care about greatly increasing the godliness they already have. They would like to have so much grace as would set them on the right hand, not on the left; on the winning and not on the losing side; but they are not concerned to have an abundant entrance if only they get into the kingdom at all. They therefore make no thoroughgoing effort to keep moving forwards, but rather avoid whatever would effectually commit them to a more devoted and self-sacrificing life. They rather repress the gracious feelings they have than seek to secure for them an increasing expression in their life. They see customs in business which they cannot approve, but they make no remonstrance. They recognize circumstances in which a word of Christian advice might be beneficial, but they do not speak it. They decline to appeal to the highest motives of those around them. They do not pray in their families. They avoid all action which might give them a character for zeal. <u>They seek to live a moderate, decent life.</u> They seek to hit the mean, and to be neither obviously godless nor to be righteous over much. They have some grace, but they do not circulate it and seek to make it more; they have a talent, but they bury it.

Of such a method of dealing with our connection with Christ, there is only one possible result. The unused talent passes from the servant who would not use it to the man who will. A landlord has two farms lying together: the one is admirably managed, the other is left almost to itself, with the least possible management, and becomes the talk of the whole countryside for poor crops and untidiness. No one asks what the landlord will do when the leases are out. It is a matter of course that he dismisses the careless tenant, and puts his farm into the hands of the skilful and diligent farmer. He enforces the great law: "To him that hath shall be given, and he shall have more abundance; but from him that hath not shall be taken even that he hath."

In the kingdom of Christ this law is self-acting. To bury our talent and so keep it as originally given is an impossibility. To have just so much grace and no more is an impossibility. It must either be circulating and so multiplying, or it ceases to be. It must grow, or it will die. You might as well try to keep your child always a child: he must either grow or die. In the physical world the law has become familiar. The unused muscle dwindles and disappears: no one needs to come and remove it; want of use removes it. The ants whose habits of life enabled them to find food without the aid of sight have gradually lost the organ of sight itself. And so is it in the spiritual world also. The unused faculty becomes extinct. Hence it is that you see some old persons absolutely callous: the time was when they had at least a capacity for believing in divine things and for choosing God as their portion, but now you would say that the very capacity is destroyed; no Godward emotion can find a place in their heart, nothing can stir a penitent thought in them. Hence it is that in your own souls you perhaps are finding that, no matter what effort you make, you cannot enter as heartily into holy services and occupations as once you did, but are finding your old joy and assurance honey-combed by unbelieving thoughts. Hence it is that the susceptibility to right feeling you had in boyhood has gone from you. You did not mean to become unfeeling, but only shrank from acting as feeling dictated. But he who blows out the flame, finds that the heat and the glow die out of themselves.

The teaching of this side of the parable, then, is alarming in the extreme. The warning it conveys proceeds not from an external voice we can defy or which may be mistaken, but from the laws of our nature; and it speaks not of an arbitrary infliction of punishment, but of results which these laws render inevitable. The unused faculty dies out. The capacities we have for loving and serving God are taken from us. That which was once possible becomes for ever impossible. The future once open to us is closed. We are permanently crippled, limited, paralyzed, deadened. Had we followed the openings given to us, had we used the talent committed to us, endless expansion and fulness of joy would have been ours, but now our chances are past. We have had our opportunity, we have for years been on probation, but now it is over for us. How gladly would a man renounce all that sin has brought him, if only he could stand again with his talent in his hand, and all life's opportunities before him. If there is one truth more than another on which the young may begin to build their life, it is this : that each time you decline a duty to which your better self prompts you, you become less capable of doing it ; and on the other hand, that each resistance to temptation, each humble and painful effort after what is good, is real growth in character, growth as real and as permanent as the growth in stature which, once attained, can never again dwindle to the size of the child.

Let us then give ear to the parable, and if we are conscious that even now we are very poor in spiritual things, let us make the most of the grace we have lest we become altogether destitute. If we are now stammering in prayer, the likelihood is we shall soon be dumb, unable to pray. If we are more frequently questioning the reality of God's interference in human affairs, and if we more freely admit doubts regarding cardinal truths, the likelihood is we shall soon disbelieve, and have the very faculty of faith paralyzed so as to be unable to perceive evidence the most weighty and conclusive. If we are letting go one by one our Christian connections, and involving ourselves more and more with worldly matters, the probability is that shortly we shall be hardened and eager worldlings. We have seen the process going on in many; why is it not to go on in ourselves? If good works and charitable employments are more a burden to us than they were, let us beware lest we wither and become fit only for the axe and the fire. As the cramped and numbed arm warns and wakens the sleeper, so let this creeping hardness that comes over our spirits awaken us, while yet there is time to chafe the dead limb to life. If yet we can summon into active life one self-denying resolution, if yet we can feel at all the constraining power of Christ's love, and can obey His voice in any one particular, if yet we can prevail upon ourselves to give up worldly and carnal ideas of life, and entertain humble and chastened desires; then let us most anxiously cherish such feelings, let us fan every good disposition into flame lest it die, let us at once circulate and invest our little remaining capital in the good works we are daily called to, that the very faculty of doing anything for God and our fellowmen may not for ever perish out of us.

In closing, it may be well to give special prominence to a truth which has throughout been implied, that <u>increased grace is its own reward</u>; or, at any rate, an essential part of it. The servant who had multiplied his talents <u>is rewarded by the possession</u> and use of these multiplied talents. He does not now get the burden of business lifted off his shoulders, and a life of ease appointed to him. This would be to reward the successful officer by depriving him of his command, as if an ample pension would compensate to a martial spirit for the want of active service and fresh opportunities of using richer experience and ampler powers. The talents gained are left in the hands that gained them, and wider opportunities for their use are afforded. This is the reward of the faithful servant of Christ; the grace he has diligently used is increased, and his opportunities continually multiply. He is always entering upon his reward; and entrance into heaven only marks the point at which his Lord expresses His approval, and raises him from a position in which his fidelity is tested to a position of rule, that is, of acknowledged trustworthiness and self-control, the position of one who has acquired an interest in the work, and who so manifestly lives for it that it is impossible any interest of his own should divert him from this. He has no other interest. His joy is his Lord's joy, joy in successfully advancing the best interests of men, joy in the sight of others made righteously happy.

This, then, is the reward Christ offers to us, a reward consisting mainly in increased ability to serve Him and forward what is good. There can be no reward more certain, for it begins here and now. Your increasing grace is your heaven begun. This is the earnest of the Spirit, the dawning of eternal day. No one need tell you that there is no heaven: the kingdom of heaven is within you. And this reward is also the best you can imagine. All other rewards would be external to yourself and separable from yourself, but this reward is within you, in your own growth in character. Not your condition alone, but you yourself are to be good. What can be better than this? What is the reward the sick man receives for his attention to every prescription of his physician and his avoidance of everything that would throw him back? His reward is that he becomes healthy. What reward has the boy for obedience and diligence and purity? His reward is that he becomes a vigorous and capable man, fit for the ampler enjoyments which the nobler activities of life bring. So says our Lord, "I am come that ye might have life, and that ye might have it more abundantly." If it be asked, what is the great inducement? what is that which makes life worth living? what is that which we can set before us as our sufficient reward and aim? the answer can only be: the inducement is that we have the sure hope of becoming satisfactory persons, of growing up to the stature and energies of perfect men, of becoming perfect as our Father is perfect, who needs no reward but delights evermore in being and doing good; who loves and is therein blessed.

www.ingramcontent.com/pod-product-compliance
Lightning Source LLC
Chambersburg PA
CBHW031928230426
43672CB00010B/1855